MISTAKES ARE LIKE FERTILISER

HOW FAILURES SHAPE US

TYSON ROBERTS

Ark House Press
arkhousepress.com

© 2025 Tyson Roberts

All rights reserved. Apart from any fair dealing for the purpose of study, research, criticism, or review, as permitted under the Copyright Act, no part may be reproduced by any process without written permission.

This book is a work of non-fiction. The figures and events mentioned have been researched based on publicly available sources. Any views or opinions expressed are solely those of the author and do not represent the views of individuals or organisations associated with the historical figures discussed.

Cataloguing in Publication Data:
Title: Mistakes Are Like Fertiliser
ISBN: 978-1-7640542-1-8 (pbk)
Subjects: PSY036000   PSYCHOLOGY / Mental Health; REL012070   RELIGION / Christian Living / Personal Growth; REL074000   RELIGION / Christian Ministry / Pastoral Resources.

Design by initiateagency.com

FOREWORD

I love self-development and personal growth. Journaling is one of my favourite things to do. Vulnerability is my happy place. It's in this space that we can truly see things for what they are, giving us the opportunity to make choices that lead to growth and transformation—like pulling out weeds and planting new seeds in preparation for a new season.

Mistakes Are Like Fertiliser is a practical handbook for personal growth, birthed from Tyson's own journey and his passion for helping others reach their best. Through this book, we encounter historical figures who made mistakes—some learned from them, while others did not. We've all made mistakes, and this book offers us a moment to reflect and decide: will our mistakes make us or break us? Will we allow them to become the very fertiliser that fuels our growth?

To help us connect with the lessons, Tyson often uses analogies, similes, and metaphors. And if I had to compare Tyson to something, he's like a Wild African Dog. While many animals have protective mothers, Wild African Dogs have deeply protective fathers. Their young are inquisitive and energetic, yet they rely entirely on their fathers for nourishment in their early weeks. These fathers chew, swallow, and regurgitate food to feed their pups, ensuring they grow strong while keeping them close to home, safe from enemies. Similarly, Tyson has a father's heart for people—

he wants to see them nourished, strengthened, and guided safely toward growth. He encourages us to use our mistakes as stepping stones rather than stumbling blocks.

As a friend who has journeyed with Tyson for over five years, I can wholeheartedly say that his passion for seeing people reach their greatest potential is genuine. He remains humble and teachable, knowing that none of us are immune to mistakes—but that none of us need to be defined or trapped by them.

So take your time with this book. Read it slowly. Reflect deeply. Have the courage to find the seeds you can plant in your own life, and fertilise them with wisdom and growth, becoming the best version of yourself.

Kath Reed – *friend and fellow personal growth enthusiast.*

ACKNOWLEDGMENTS

First and foremost, I want to thank God – for His endless grace, and for somehow turning my many mistakes into chances to grow, rather than total disasters. That's been nothing short of a miracle.

To my incredible wife – thank you for sticking with me through every misstep, wrong turn, and wild idea that popped into my head. You are the heart of everything I do. Without your love, patience, and much-needed sense of humour, this book – and honestly, my life – would be a lot messier.

To my kids – thank you for reminding me, every single day, that no one gets it right all the time. Watching you figure things out (and sometimes mess things up) has taught me more than I could ever put into words. You've been my greatest teachers, whether you know it or not.

To my friends and family – thanks for being my sounding board, my support crew, and occasionally, the unwilling participants in my less-than-perfect plans. Your encouragement (and your cheeky banter) has meant more than you probably realise.

To everyone who's been part of my journey – especially those who had front-row seats to my mess-ups – thank you. You've helped me see that mistakes really can be like fertiliser: smelly, yes, but full of potential. Your wisdom, kindness, and just showing up when it counted has shaped me in all the best ways.

MISTAKES ARE LIKE FERTILISER

And finally, to you – the reader. Thanks for picking up this book. I hope that somewhere in these pages, you find a bit of humour, a few insights, and maybe even a shift in how you see your own mistakes. They might just grow into something good.

A NOTE TO THE READER

Let's be real – a whole book about mistakes? Sounds a bit heavy, doesn't it? I get it. I've been in that same loop – stuffing up, repeating the same patterns, wondering if I'd ever figure it out. And that voice in your head? The one that whispers, *"You're too late. Too far gone. Maybe you're just not the kind of person who gets it right."* Yeah, I know that one too. It's exhausting.

That's part of why I wrote this – not because I've got it all worked out (spoiler: I absolutely don't), but because I know what it's like to fall flat and still want to grow from it. Over time, I've learned that mistakes don't have to be the end of the story. They can sting, sure – but they can also shift us, stretch us, shape us. If we let them.

This book isn't meant to be read cover to cover like a novel. You'll probably get more out of it if you dip in and out – stop when something grabs you, skip bits that don't quite fit, come back to a part later when it hits different. Think of it more like a wander through someone else's messy garden. You'll find what speaks to you.

You won't find any lectures in here. No life-coach vibes or five-step plans. Just stories – some from history, some from everyday life, a few from the cracks in between – that show how mistakes can shape us, shake us, and sometimes even wake us up. My hope is that somewhere in all of this, you'll catch a glimpse of yourself. Or someone you care about.

MISTAKES ARE LIKE FERTILISER

So, if you've ever felt like everyone else has it together except you – you're in good company. None of us really do. But maybe, just maybe, this book helps you see your mess in a new light – not as a failure, but as the fertiliser for something better.

TABLE OF CONTENTS

Introduction 1
Mistakes are like fertiliser – you can choose to let them grow you, or kill you.

Part 1: Catastrophic Failures – The Seeds of Destruction 9
In every great story of success, there are often darker tales of those who failed to rise above their mistakes. For some, these mistakes were not mere missteps but catastrophic decisions that led to their undoing.

Planting Stage 1: Ned Kelly – The Unyielding Rebel 13
Quote: "Such is life" – Ned Kelly
Mistake: Violence as resistance against authority.

Planting Stage 2: Napoleon Bonaparte – The Conqueror's Hubris ... 23
Quote: "The greatest danger occurs at the moment of victory" – Napoleon Bonaparte
Mistake: Overconfident invasion of Russia.

Planting Stage 3: Richard Nixon – The Scandal that Shook the Nation 33
Quote: "People have got to know whether or not their president is a crook. Well, I am not a crook!" – Richard Nixon

Mistake: The Watergate scandal and cover-up.

Planting Stage 4: Diego Maradona – The Brilliance and the Downfall 44
Quote: "I made mistakes, and I paid for them" – Diego Maradona
Mistake: Drug addiction amidst football greatness.

Planting Stage 5: King Ludwig II of Bavaria – The Dreamer's Downfall 54
Quote: "I wish to remain an eternal enigma to myself and others" – King Ludwig II
Mistake: Extravagant castle building at the expense of his kingdom.

Part 2: Setbacks – Lessons in Recovery and Resilience 65
Not every mistake leads to complete destruction. For some, missteps leave deep wounds but not defeat. These individuals experienced partial failures that carried heavy consequences.

Planting Stage 6: Elon Musk – The Visionary Who Overpromised .. 67
Quote: "When something is important enough, you do it even if the odds are not in your favour" – Elon Musk
Mistake: Overpromising and erratic public behaviour.

Planting Stage 7: Mark Zuckerberg – The Man Who Connected the World and Exposed Its Privacy 77
Quote: "The question isn't 'What do we want to know about people?' It's 'What do people want to tell about themselves?'" – Mark Zuckerberg
Mistake: Mishandling user data, leading to the Cambridge Analytica scandal.

Planting Stage 8: Steve Jobs – The Visionary's Fall and Return 87
Quote: "Sometimes life is going to hit you in the head with a brick. Don't lose faith" – Steve Jobs
Mistake: Failing to collaborate, leading to his ousting from Apple.

Planting Stage 9: Empress Dowager Cixi – The Empress Who Resisted Change 97
Quote: "I have often wished I had been born in another age, a time of less strife and fewer worries" – Empress Dowager Cixi
Mistake: Resisting modernisation during a critical period for China.

Planting Stage 10: Marie Curie – The Cost of Dedication 107
Quote: "The way of progress was neither swift nor easy" – Marie Curie
Mistake: Health risks from prolonged radiation exposure.

Part 3: Inspirational Turnarounds – Seeds of Redemption 117
In the face of failure, some rise to incredible heights. This section looks at those who turned their mistakes into opportunities for growth and lasting change.

Planting Stage 11: Akio Morita – Betting Everything on a Bold Vision 119
Quote: "Don't be afraid to make a mistake. But make sure you don't make the same mistake twice" – Akio Morita
Turnaround: Founding Sony and recovering from early business failures.

Planting Stage 12: Nelson Mandela – The Power of Forgiveness 130
Quote: "Resentment is like drinking poison and then hoping it will kill your enemies" – Nelson Mandela
Turnaround: From violent resistance to peaceful leadership.

**Planting Stage 13: Winston Churchill – The Man Who
Bounded Back from Failure** 140
Quote: "Success is not final; failure is not fatal: it is the courage to continue that counts" – Winston Churchill
Turnaround: Bouncing back after the Gallipoli disaster in WWI to lead Britain in WWII.

**Planting Stage 14: Oskar Schindler – The Profiteer Who
Became a Hero** 151
Quote: "Whoever saves one life, saves the world entire" – Talmud
Turnaround: From war profiteer to Holocaust saviour.

Planting Stage 15: Alfred Nobel – The Legacy of Redemption 161
Quote: "I wish to leave behind me a world that is better than the one I found" – Alfred Nobel
Turnaround: From the inventor of TNT to establishing the Nobel Peace Prize.

Conclusion: Cultivating Your Own Growth 173
Mistakes can either bury you or become the very seeds of growth. The stories in this book show that with the right perspective, even the gravest mistakes can be turned into opportunities for learning, redemption, and personal development.

INTRODUCTION

"Mistakes are like fertiliser – you can choose to let them grow you, or kill you"

Let's face it – everyone stuffs up. Doesn't matter who you are, where you're from, or what you do – mistakes are part of being human. Some are small and stay with us quietly. Others? They explode outwards, leaving a trail that stretches far and wide. But no matter the size, the real question isn't *if* we'll mess up. It's what we do *after* we do.

When I first said, "mistakes are like fertiliser," it was one of those lightbulb moments. The kind that changes how you see things. Fertiliser's got all the good stuff that helps things grow – but used the wrong way, it can burn through roots and kill what you're trying to nurture. Mistakes are a lot like that. Handled with care, they feed growth. Ignored or mishandled, they scorch everything around them.

Take a moment to think about a mistake you've made recently. Did you grow from it? Or are you still dragging it behind you? Keep that in the back of your mind as you read – it might just shift something.

This book dives into mistakes – big ones, quiet ones, public ones, private ones. We'll look at how people have handled them – or not – and what we can learn from the fallout. You'll hear about folks like Winston

Churchill, whose battlefield blunders shaped his future leadership, and Diego Maradona, whose personal struggles were just as defining as his talent. These aren't just historical footnotes – they're mirrors, if we're willing to look.

Why Look at Mistakes?

We live in a world that glorifies success and shuns failure. From polished social media feeds to carefully curated professional resumes, we're often shown a version of life that appears flawless – a narrative where success comes easily, and mistakes are swept under the rug. But beneath every great achievement lies a trail of missteps, setbacks, and hard lessons learned. The truth is that failure is not the enemy of success; it is often its foundation.

If we look closer, we'll see that every successful person has faced failure in some form. These moments of defeat, frustration, or disappointment, are not anomalies – they're universal experiences that test our resolve and reveal what we're truly capable of. Consider Thomas Edison, who famously said, "I have not failed. I've just found 10,000 ways that won't work." Edison's perseverance turned those '10,000 ways' into one of the most important inventions of modern times: the electric light bulb. His story is a powerful reminder that failure is not a dead end – it is part of the journey.

Mistakes, while painful, are invaluable teachers. They show us what doesn't work and, in doing so, brings us closer to what does. They force us to question our assumptions, rethink our strategies, and dig deeper into our own potential. When approached with the right mindset, mistakes have the power to transform us, sharpening our focus and strengthening our character.

What if you could see your mistakes through that same lens? What if, instead of seeing failure as an indictment of your abilities, you saw it as a stepping stone toward growth? How might that shift in perspective change the way you approach challenges, setbacks, and even your greatest ambitions?

This book isn't about celebrating failure for its own sake. It's about recognising the powerful role mistakes can play in shaping who we become. Mistakes are not roadblocks – they're guideposts, pointing us toward paths we might not have otherwise considered. They're opportunities to reflect, adapt, and emerge stronger than before. But this only happens if we're willing to confront our failures honestly, and embrace the lessons they offer.

As you turn the pages of this book, I invite you to see your mistakes as more than moments of regret. They're moments to learn, to grow, and to redefine what's possible. Mistakes are not something to fear; they're essential ingredients in the recipe for resilience and success. So, what will you do with yours? Will you let them hold you back, or will you let them guide you toward the person you're meant to become?

Ask yourself: What would happen if you stopped fearing mistakes and started using them as tools for progress?

The Hidden Potential in Setbacks

Setbacks often feel like the end of the road, moments that force us to question our abilities and our goals. But what if they weren't the end at all? What if they were detours, redirecting us toward a destination we couldn't yet see?

Consider Steve Jobs, whose ousting from Apple in 1985 seemed like the ultimate failure. At the time, Jobs was devastated – removed from the company he had co-founded and defined. But instead of succumbing to despair, he used this setback as an opportunity to reflect, innovate, and grow. His ventures with NeXT and Pixar not only became successes in their own right, but also provided the tools and vision that would define Apple's resurgence when he returned in 1997. What appeared to be a devastating failure was, in hindsight, the turning point that led to his most iconic achievements.

Setbacks, whether personal or professional, force us to pause and recalibrate. They challenge us to think differently and uncover new strengths. A failed relationship might teach you resilience, while a career stumble could reveal a path you hadn't considered.

Ask yourself: How might a recent setback in your life be pointing you toward something better? What opportunities or lessons could it uncover?

Planting the seed: Reflect on a recent setback and write down one lesson it has taught you. Then, identify a single actionable step you can take to embrace this new direction.

The Purpose of This Book

In the chapters that follow, we'll explore the lives of individuals – some famous, some lesser-known – who made profound mistakes. These are people who stood at pivotal crossroads in their lives, where decisions, made in moments of fear, ambition, or misjudgement, led to outcomes they hadn't foreseen. We'll look at what went wrong, why it happened and, most importantly, how these mistakes became defining moments, forcing them to adapt, grow, or, in some cases, face the consequences of not doing so.

This is more than a history lesson – it's a toolkit for reflection and growth. Each story is a window into the complexities of human nature, the circumstances that lead to failure, and the resilience it takes to rise again. By reflecting on their stories, you'll gain insights into handling your own challenges – whether it's navigating a career setback, overcoming personal doubts, or managing relationships. These are not just tales of the past; they are lessons for the present and blueprints for building a better future.

INTRODUCTION

For each figure, we'll delve into the historical and personal contexts surrounding their mistakes. What external pressures did they face? What internal struggles may have clouded their judgment? And how did their decisions ripple outward to affect those around them? By examining these layers, we'll extract lessons that resonate in our own lives. Reflecting on the past isn't just about understanding it – it's about using its wisdom to shape who we are and the choices we make moving forward.

Ask yourself: What would you have done differently in their shoes? How does this apply to your own life today? Could the lessons embedded in their journeys help you avoid similar pitfalls, or approach your own challenges with greater clarity?

This isn't a passive read – it's an invitation to reflect on your own story, to consider how the decisions and mistakes of others can illuminate your path, and to equip yourself with the tools needed to grow from your experiences. Their turning points could inspire your own. Are you ready to step into their stories and discover how they might transform yours?

Turning Mistakes into Strengths

One of the most transformative lessons from the stories in this book is that mistakes can reveal our hidden strengths. These moments, while painful, often act as mirrors, reflecting back resilience, creativity, or adaptability we didn't realise we had.

Take Alfred Nobel, for example. His invention of dynamite revolutionised industries, but also brought devastation to warfare. Branded as a "merchant of death", Nobel faced the moral weight of his mistakes. Instead of allowing regret to define him, he used it as a catalyst for change. His decision to create the Nobel Prizes transformed his legacy into one of peace, progress, and innovation. What appeared to be his greatest failure became the foundation of his greatest strength.

Ask yourself: What strengths have your mistakes revealed about you? How can you use those strengths to navigate future challenges?

Planting the seed: Reflect on a mistake and identify one strength it uncovered. Write down how you can apply that strength to overcome a current obstacle or achieve a personal goal.

Breaking the Cycle

Despite the countless lessons history has to offer, humanity continues to repeat the same mistakes. Time and again, empires crumble, economies collapse, and relationships fracture – all due to errors that could have been avoided if we had only learned from the past.

Yet, when it comes to learning from our mistakes, we often fall into the same traps of denial and pride. Why is this? Is it fear of being vulnerable? Or the belief that acknowledging failure makes us weak? These are questions we'll explore together.

Ask yourself: What patterns do you see in your own life that keep repeating? How can learning from past missteps help you break free and move forward?

Planting the seed: Identify one recurring mistake in your life. Write down a lesson you've learned from it and a concrete action you can take to avoid repeating it in the future.

INTRODUCTION

My Challenge to You

My hope for you, the reader of this book, is to break free from the cycle of fear, avoidance, and perfectionism that so often surrounds mistakes. In a society that values curated success over genuine growth, I challenge you to step into a different narrative – one where your mistakes are not something to be hidden or denied but embraced as vital tools for transformation.

Reject the culture that equates perfection with value, and instead embrace a new kind of strength – one that comes from vulnerability, self-awareness, and the courage to face your flaws head-on. True growth isn't about avoiding failure; it's about having the resilience to learn from it, the humility to admit when you're wrong, and the boldness to keep moving forward despite the setbacks.

Don't let your errors define you, or worse, doom your future. Be a pioneer in a world that desperately needs authenticity. By owning your mistakes, you take control of your narrative, turning moments of failure into stepping stones for success. Your openness to learn and adapt could inspire others to do the same, creating a ripple effect of honesty, growth, and progress.

Ask yourself: Are you ready to embrace your mistakes and let them become the fertiliser for your growth? What would happen if, instead of hiding from your errors, you chose to confront them, learn from them, and use them as fuel for transformation?

This is your chance to redefine failure – not as an endpoint but as a critical part of the journey. It's your opportunity to reframe the challenges and setbacks you've faced and turn them into the foundation for your greatest achievements.

MISTAKES ARE LIKE FERTILISER

The individuals in this book faced moments of doubt, moments of regret, and moments of failure, but what sets many of them apart is their willingness to rise again. You, too, have that ability. Take the lessons you'll encounter in these pages and apply them to your own story. Use them to reimagine what's possible, and to create a legacy rooted in growth and resilience.

The true pioneers of tomorrow will not be those who avoid mistakes, but those who dare to own them, learn from them, and grow beyond them. If you can do that, you won't just break the mould – you'll redefine it entirely.

So, I leave you with this challenge: Will you let your mistakes weigh you down, or will you use them as the fertiliser for a life of growth, authenticity, and impact? The choice is yours, and it starts now.

PART 1
CATASTROPHIC FAILURES – THE SEEDS OF DESTRUCTION

In every great story of success, there are often darker tales of those who failed to rise above their mistakes. For some, these mistakes were not mere missteps but catastrophic decisions that led to their undoing. These individuals had the potential for greatness, yet they were brought down by poor choices, unchecked ambition, or a refusal to learn from their errors.

In this section, we delve into the lives of five figures whose mistakes consumed them. They were gifted with talents, opportunities, and platforms most can only dream of, yet their decisions led them down paths of destruction. Their falls were monumental, leaving ripples that affected not just their own lives, but those around them and, in some cases, the world.

From Ned Kelly's violent rebellion to King Ludwig II's financial ruin, these stories reveal the tragic consequences of unchecked mistakes.

These individuals represent the worst-case scenarios of failure. Their stories show how ego, hubris, and bad choices, when left unchecked, can dismantle even the brightest futures. Failure, as we see through them, often doesn't come from external forces alone, but from within – growing when we refuse to confront our flaws, acknowledge our mistakes, or seek redemption.

It's a sobering reminder that brilliance and talent, no matter how great, cannot shield us from the consequences of poor decisions.

Each story illustrates how a singular focus or unaddressed flaw can lead to disaster:

- **Ned Kelly**, the unyielding rebel, who believed violence was the only way to resist authority, leaving behind a legacy of bloodshed and tragedy.
- **Napoleon Bonaparte**, the brilliant conqueror, who was undone by his overconfidence, leading to disaster during his ill-fated invasion of Russia.
- **Richard Nixon**, a powerful leader, who saw his presidency crumble under the weight of the Watergate scandal, as the cover-up became worse than the crime.
- **Diego Maradona**, a football legend, who let drug addiction tarnish his brilliance on the field, becoming a cautionary tale for greatness lost to personal struggles.
- **King Ludwig II**, a dreamer, who sacrificed the stability of his kingdom for extravagant castles, leaving a legacy of beauty built on ruin.

While their mistakes are grave, they offer invaluable lessons for the rest of us. As you read these stories, consider how the seeds of their downfall were sown. What might have happened if they had chosen differently? And, more importantly, how can you apply these lessons to your own life, ensuring you don't repeat the same patterns?

CATASTROPHIC FAILURES – THE SEEDS OF DESTRUCTION

Before you begin, think of a moment in your life when a decision or mindset led you toward a negative outcome. What might you have done differently? Hold that thought as you explore these stories, and let their lessons guide your reflections.

These cautionary tales reveal that brilliance and talent are not enough to shield anyone from the consequences of poor decisions. But they also serve as powerful reminders of the importance of humility, accountability, and the courage to change – before it's too late.

What seeds are you planting in your own life today? Are they ones that will nourish your future – or ones that may grow into obstacles?

PLANTING STAGE 1

Ned Kelly – The Unyielding Rebel

Quote: "Such is life" – Ned Kelly

Image: *"Ned Kelly at Bay" by Tom Carrington, 1880.*
Public domain via Wikimedia Commons.

Before You Read:

If you've ever admired someone for standing up to authority—even when it got messy—Ned Kelly's story will feel familiar. But what makes a rebel heroic versus self-destructive? You might compare him to Mandela (Chapter 12), who also fought oppression but chose a different path. Or to Richard Nixon (Chapter 3), where defiance turned inward and secretive instead of loud and public.

Breaking Ground: The Man Behind the Iron Helmet

Ned Kelly is a name well-known in Australian history, often associated with rebellion. Born in 1854 into a poor family, Kelly grew up facing hardship, constantly in trouble with the law. At a time when the British colonial government enforced harsh rules that affected the poor more than anyone else, Kelly's frustration with authority grew.

To some, he became a folk hero – Australia's Robin Hood – standing up against injustice. To others, he was a dangerous criminal whose refusal to follow the law brought chaos and bloodshed. Kelly's life was shaped by difficulty, loss, and anger toward what he saw as a corrupt system.

However, his unwillingness to compromise, and his choice to fight authority at every turn, eventually led to his downfall. His final stand, wearing homemade armour during the famous Glenrowan shootout, became the defining moment of his life – and his ultimate mistake.

Kelly's story challenges us to consider: when is resistance heroic, and when does it become destructive?

Sowing the Seeds of Mistake

Ned Kelly's mistake wasn't just in fighting for justice – it was in believing that violence was the only way to achieve it. His anger toward the system was understandable; he grew up watching the police target his family and others like them. But instead of seeking peaceful solutions, Kelly chose violence.

As a young man, Kelly had several run-ins with the law, which only deepened his hatred for authority. His family's poverty, and Irish Catholic background, often put them in conflict with the British authorities.

Kelly was arrested several times for minor offenses and, in his mind, this was proof that the police were out to get him. But instead of stepping back and seeking lawful ways to fight the system, Kelly embraced a dangerous "us versus them" mentality. This mindset, fuelled by anger, became the seed of his downfall. How often do we let emotion cloud our judgment in the heat of the moment?

Reaping What was Sown

The Glenrowan siege was a disaster. Kelly had a plan to derail a police train, but it failed, and the police surrounded the hotel where he and his gang had taken refuge. In the chaotic shootout that followed, Kelly was shot multiple times in the legs and captured, while his gang members were killed.

His armour, which he had believed would make him invincible because it was 4.5mm to 6mm thick and weighed 44kg, became a burden that contributed to his defeat. Kelly's belief in his own invincibility – like his approach to rebellion – was flawed. Sometimes, the very things we think will protect us can become our greatest obstacles.

After his capture, Kelly was put on trial for murder. Despite public debates about his legacy as a folk hero, he was sentenced to hang. His execution in November 1880 marked the end of his rebellion, and the failure of his violent approach to justice.

Kelly's story is a reminder that even just causes can be undermined by the wrong methods. What legacy will you leave behind – one of constructive change, or destructive defiance?

Harvesting the Lessons

Ned Kelly's life and eventual downfall highlight the consequences of unchecked defiance, misplaced loyalty, and the failure to balance courage with strategy. While his rebellion against authority made him a folk hero, his decision to confront police in an iron suit at Glenrowan sealed his fate, leading to his capture and execution.

Kelly's story reminds us of the fine line between bravery and recklessness. Passionate resistance without careful planning can lead to unintended consequences, no matter how justified the cause.

His legacy underscores the importance of standing up for one's beliefs – but also the need for strategy, foresight, and reflection to avoid needless escalation.

These lessons resonate today in both personal and societal contexts, encouraging us to temper boldness with wisdom, and to channel our convictions toward thoughtful, meaningful actions.

Here are three scenarios to reflect on, with reflections to help apply these lessons to your own life:

Scenario 1: Fighting for the Right Cause in the Wrong Way

You're deeply committed to a project at work and feel frustrated when colleagues don't share your urgency. To push things forward, you raise your voice or send pointed emails, but later wonder if it's helping or hindering progress.

Reflection Questions:

- What emotions or beliefs are driving your response in this situation?

- How do your methods influence others' willingness to support your cause?

- What alternative actions might foster collaboration and understanding instead of resistance?

Scenario 2: Letting Anger Drive Decisions

You're in an argument with a close friend, and a misunderstanding causes tempers to flare. In the heat of the moment, you say something you later regret, escalating the conflict rather than resolving it.

Reflection Questions:

- How often does anger influence your actions in challenging situations?

- What signals might help you recognise when anger is taking control?

- How could stepping back in this moment change the tone of the conversation or its outcome?

Scenario 3: Considering Long-Term Consequences

You're faced with a decision to call out someone in a public setting for their behaviour. While it feels justified in the moment, you later wonder how the approach might affect your relationship or reputation.

Reflection Questions:

- When you make decisions, how often do you think about their ripple effects?

- Are your choices building bridges or creating barriers for the future?

- What steps could you take to balance addressing the issue with preserving long-term trust?

Final Reflection:

These scenarios ask you to pause and examine your methods, emotions, and long-term perspective. As you reflect, consider:

- Are your actions creating understanding and growth, or are they sparking unnecessary conflict?
- What adjustments could bring you closer to the outcomes you truly want to achieve?

Tilling the Soil of Reflection

Ned Kelly's story invites reflection on the dangers of rigid thinking, and the escalation of conflict. His choices, born of anger and a deep sense of injustice, highlight how defiance can sometimes overshadow the cause it seeks to champion. By relying on violence as his primary means of resistance, Kelly alienated potential supporters and cemented his reputation as an outlaw rather than a reformer.

His life challenges us to consider the cost of unchecked anger and unyielding defiance. While his grievances against the system were valid, his approach ultimately led to his downfall. Kelly's story serves as a cautionary reminder that how we choose to fight for what we believe in can shape not only our outcomes but also our legacy.

Do you let emotions like anger or frustration cloud your judgment? How might a more thoughtful, adaptable approach lead to better outcomes?

Breaking New Ground

Have you ever seen how farmers prepare their fields for planting? They don't just toss seeds onto hard-packed ground and hope for the best. Instead, they till the soil, breaking through the hardened surface so the seeds can take root and thrive. Our emotions and mindsets are no different. Anger and frustration can harden us, making it difficult for anything new to grow.

But here's the thing: those emotions – if we take the time to work through them – can become the foundation for something transformative. It's not about ignoring or suppressing them; it's about digging deep, softening the rough patches, and redirecting that energy into something constructive.

Think about a time when you let anger or frustration take over. Did it help you achieve your goal, or did it leave you feeling stuck or worse off?

Like hardened soil, these emotions need attention – they need to be tilled and worked through to make way for growth.

Ned Kelly's story offers a powerful lesson. His fight against injustice was rooted in valid grievances, but his reliance on violence and rigid thinking limited his potential to create lasting change.

What if he had paused, reassessed, and channelled his passion into more collaborative and constructive methods? His legacy might have been one of reform rather than rebellion.

Cultivating Growth

Ned Kelly's story reflects the dangers of letting anger and rigid thinking dictate our actions. While his fight against perceived injustice made him a symbol of defiance, his reliance on violence ultimately undermined his cause and led to his downfall.

His life invites us to examine how we channel our frustrations and pursue justice with intention and clarity.

Key Takeaways:

- **Anger Needs a Channel**: While anger at injustice can fuel action, untempered anger often leads to destructive outcomes. Finding constructive ways to express frustration is essential for meaningful progress.
- **Evaluate Your Methods**: The way you pursue your goals is as important as the goals themselves. Ensure your actions align with the values and outcomes you aim to uphold.
- **Adaptability Over Rigidity**: Sticking too firmly to one method – especially when it proves ineffective – can result in failure. Flexibility opens the door to better strategies and outcomes.

True growth isn't about standing firm no matter what. It's about knowing when to pause, reflect, and adapt. It's about balancing conviction with flexibility and channelling your emotions into actions that align with your long-term values.

Breaking new ground isn't easy – it's messy, uncomfortable, and often requires us to let go of old ways of thinking. But it's also necessary. By loosening the hardened emotions and mindsets that hold us back, we create space for something truly transformative.

So, here's the challenge: What hardened soil exists in your life right now? Where do frustration or rigid thinking prevent growth? And what steps can you take to till that soil and create the conditions for something new to flourish?

Growth doesn't happen by accident. It happens when we prepare ourselves for it – one thoughtful action at a time.

PLANTING STAGE 2

Napoleon Bonaparte – The Conqueror's Hubris

Quote: "The greatest danger occurs at the moment of victory"
– Napoleon Bonaparte

Image: Napoleon Bonaparte by Paul Delaroche. Public domain via Wikimedia Commons.

Before You Read:

If you're drawn to ambition—the kind that won't quit—Napoleon is a towering figure. But what happens when momentum becomes blind faith? If you've read about Elon Musk (Chapter 6) or Steve Jobs (Chapter 8), you'll see how visionary thinking walks a fine line between bold and brittle.

Breaking Ground: The Rise of Napoleon

Napoleon Bonaparte was one of the most brilliant military minds in history, a man who reshaped the map of Europe and seemed destined for greatness.

Born in 1769 on the island of Corsica, Napoleon's rise from a modest background to Emperor of France was a testament to his ambition, tactical genius, and relentless drive. During the chaos of the French Revolution, he used his military talents to secure victory after victory, eventually taking control of France and crowning himself Emperor in 1804.

Under his reign, Napoleon expanded the French Empire to its peak, toppling monarchs, redrawing borders, and making reforms that would leave a lasting mark on Europe. His Napoleonic Code reformed legal systems, and his modernisation of education and infrastructure showed his leadership beyond the battlefield. At the height of his power, Napoleon seemed unstoppable – until he made his greatest mistake.

The Ground from Which It Grew: The State of Europe

By 1812, Napoleon was at the height of his power. His empire stretched across Europe, from Spain in the west to the borders of Russia in the east.

However, his aggressive expansionism had made him many enemies. Great Britain, Austria, Prussia, and Russia had formed alliances against him, determined to halt his ambitions. Napoleon responded by waging war after war, confident that his military prowess would continue to bring him victory.

While the French people, tired of constant conflict, still saw Napoleon as a hero due to his victories, the strain of war was beginning to show. His enemies were growing stronger, and his empire was overstretched. But Napoleon's growing belief in his invincibility – and his inability to recognise the limits of his power – set him on a collision course with disaster.

Sowing the Seeds of Mistake

Napoleon's fatal mistake came in 1812 when he decided to invade Russia. This wasn't just a tactical error – it was a reflection of his growing arrogance. By this time, Napoleon had grown so used to winning that he believed his Grande Armée, over 600,000 strong, was invincible.

The Russian Tsar, Alexander I, had grown tired of Napoleon's dominance in Europe and refused to support the Continental System, Napoleon's plan to block British trade in Europe. Viewing this as a direct challenge to his authority, Napoleon marched his army deep into Russia, expecting a quick and decisive victory.

However, Napoleon severely underestimated the challenges ahead. Russia's vast, uncharted terrain, and brutal winters, presented obstacles that no amount of military genius could overcome. Worse, the Russians employed scorched-earth tactics, burning their own cities and crops to deny the French supplies. Napoleon, blinded by his belief in his destiny, marched his army deeper into the unforgiving landscape.

When he finally engaged the Russians at the Battle of Borodino in September 1812, the French emerged victorious – but it was a hollow victory. Both sides suffered heavy casualties, and the Russian army retreated, leaving Napoleon no closer to his goal. When he reached Moscow, he found the city abandoned and in flames, offering no shelter or supplies for his army.

Have you ever been so confident in your abilities that you overlooked potential risks? Napoleon's story challenges us to stay humble in the face of success. Sometimes, the greatest victories lie not in pressing forward but in knowing when to pause and reassess.

Reaping What Was Sown

The retreat from Moscow stands as one of history's greatest military disasters. Weakened by hunger, disease, and the freezing cold, Napoleon's once-mighty Grande Armée was relentlessly harassed by Russian forces.

Of the more than 600,000 soldiers who marched into Russia, fewer than 100,000 made it back to France. Napoleon's overconfidence, combined with his refusal to adapt to the realities of the campaign, had led to catastrophic failure.

The consequences of the failed Russian campaign were immediate. Emboldened by his defeat, Napoleon's enemies formed a new coalition against him. By 1814, his forces were defeated on multiple fronts, and his empire was crumbling. Forced to abdicate, Napoleon was exiled to the island of Elba.

But Napoleon's ambition didn't die with his exile. In 1815, he staged a dramatic return to France, regaining power during the Hundred Days war. However, his comeback was short-lived. At the Battle of Waterloo, Napoleon was decisively defeated. This time, he was exiled to the distant island of St Helena, where he spent the remainder of his life in isolation.

Napoleon's decision to invade Russia not only cost him his empire, but it also tarnished his legacy as a military genius. His inability to recognise the limits of his power, and his refusal to adapt to changing circumstances, serve as a powerful cautionary tale.

Harvesting the Lessons

Napoleon Bonaparte's disastrous invasion of Russia serves as a timeless warning about the dangers of overconfidence, poor planning, and underestimating external challenges. His decision to march into Russia, without adequately preparing for the harsh winter or logistical difficulties, decimated his army and marked the beginning of his downfall.

Napoleon's story illustrates that even the most capable and powerful individuals can fall victim to their own hubris. Ambition is a valuable trait, but unchecked ambition that ignores risks or dismisses the advice of others can lead to devastating consequences.

These lessons remain relevant today, urging us to approach challenges with humility, preparation, and a clear understanding of our limitations. Napoleon's failure teaches us that confidence must be tempered with strategy, and that even the boldest plans require careful thought and execution to succeed.

Here are three scenarios to reflect on, with reflections to help apply these lessons to your own life:

Scenario 1: Overconfidence in Familiar Approaches

You've recently received praise for completing a major project, and now you're tackling a similar task. Confident in your prior methods, you begin working without revisiting whether the new project's requirements differ. Midway through, you notice things aren't progressing as smoothly as before.

Reflection Questions:

- How much are you relying on past successes without adapting to current circumstances?

- What signals might indicate that a different approach is needed?

- How could stepping back to reassess improve the outcome?

NAPOLEON BONAPARTE – THE CONQUEROR'S HUBRIS

Scenario 2: Ignoring Advice or Feedback

A close friend or colleague offers constructive criticism about how you've been handling a recurring issue, but you dismiss their concerns. Later, you notice the problem persists, leaving you wondering if their perspective could have helped.

Reflection Questions:

- How do you typically respond to feedback, especially when it challenges your plans?

- Who in your life might have insights that could broaden your perspective?

- What might change if you practiced active listening and tried applying their advice?

Scenario 3: Pushing Through Without Pausing

You're working toward a personal goal but notice the process isn't yielding the results you hoped for. Instead of re-evaluating your strategy, you push harder, hoping persistence alone will lead to success. However, the obstacles grow larger, leaving you frustrated.

Reflection Questions:

- When things aren't going as planned, how often do you pause to reflect before pushing forward?

- What's one area where you might benefit from stepping back and reassessing?

- How could reevaluating your approach help you achieve your goals more effectively?

Final Reflection:

As you think about these scenarios, consider:

- Are your decisions driven by clarity and adaptability, or by a desire to repeat past successes?
- How might humility, self-awareness, and a willingness to pause lead to better outcomes in your life?

Tilling the Soil of Reflection

When faced with challenges, how do you respond? Do you, like Napoleon, rely on past successes and press forward, even when the circumstances demand a new approach? Or are you willing to step back, reflect, and adapt to the realities of the situation?

Napoleon's story challenges us to examine how we handle setbacks and uncertainty. Do we let overconfidence or pride blind us to alternative solutions? Or can we pause, reassess, and choose a better path forward?

Breaking New Ground

Imagine a brilliant chess player at the peak of their game, confident they can anticipate every move their opponent might make. But what happens when their confidence blinds them to the unexpected? Napoleon Bonaparte, one of history's greatest strategists, found himself in this exact position – convinced of his invincibility, only to be undone by miscalculations and the forces he underestimated.

Take his invasion of Russia: Napoleon believed his army's strength and his leadership could overcome any challenge. But he overlooked the severity of the Russian winter, the resilience of his opponents, and the logistical limitations of his campaign. The result? A catastrophic loss that not only decimated his forces but marked the turning point of his downfall.

Like a chess player who overextends, Napoleon's story serves as a reminder that unchecked confidence and rigid thinking can blind us to risks and opportunities. Have you ever been so convinced of your ability to succeed that you ignored advice, warning signs, or alternative approaches? How did it play out?

Cultivating Growth

Napoleon's story reflects the dangers of pride and overconfidence. While his ambition and strategic brilliance propelled him to incredible heights, his downfall illustrates the importance of humility, self-awareness, and adaptability in sustaining success.

Key Takeaways:

- **Confidence vs Overconfidence**: Confidence is a powerful tool, but unchecked, it can evolve into arrogance. Regularly assess whether your decisions are informed by reality or inflated by ego.
- **Learn From Setbacks**: Even the best plans can fail. The ability to adapt, reevaluate, and learn from mistakes is critical for long-term growth.
- **Embrace Counsel**: Great leaders don't act alone. Surround yourself with advisors who challenge your ideas and offer perspectives you might have overlooked.

True growth isn't about believing you're invincible – it's about Recognising your vulnerabilities and learning from them. Napoleon's legacy teaches us that brilliance alone isn't enough; it must be tempered with humility, flexibility, and a willingness to listen to others.

Here's the challenge: Are there areas in your life where confidence may have crossed into overconfidence? Are you ignoring advice, dismissing alternative strategies, or pushing ahead without fully assessing the risks?

Growth isn't about avoiding ambition – it's about channelling it wisely, with humility as your compass.

PLANTING STAGE 3

Richard Nixon – The Scandal that Shook the Nation

Quote: "People have got to know whether or not their president is a crook. Well, I am not a crook!"
– Richard Nixon

Image: Richard Nixon. Public domain, U.S. National Archives via Wikimedia Commons.

Before You Read:

Nixon's downfall wasn't the crime—it was the cover-up. If you've already explored Mark Zuckerberg (Chapter 7), you'll spot echoes of damage done not by intent but by secrecy and delayed accountability. Both stories ask: how much trust can be rebuilt after it's broken?

Breaking Ground: The Rise of Richard Nixon

Richard Nixon's rise in American politics was marked by tenacity, resilience, and ambition. Born in 1913 in California, he came from humble beginnings and worked his way up through the political ranks.

By 1953, he was Vice President of the United States under Dwight D Eisenhower, and though he lost the 1960 presidential race to John F Kennedy, Nixon was not one to give up. His perseverance led to a remarkable comeback, culminating in his victory in the 1968 presidential election.

As president, Nixon navigated a nation torn by the Vietnam War and social upheaval. His diplomatic achievements, including the groundbreaking visit to China, and easing tensions with the Soviet Union, solidified his reputation as a shrewd statesman.

At one point, Nixon seemed poised to leave an indelible mark on history as one of America's most accomplished presidents.

But behind this image of success lay deep-seated insecurities, and a growing mistrust of his political enemies. These internal struggles led to poor decisions that would ultimately result in his downfall. The scandal that would define his legacy began with a seemingly small crime – a break-in at the Watergate complex.

The Ground from Which It Grew: The Political Landscape of the 1970s

The early 1970s were a period of intense political and social change in the United States. The Vietnam War had divided the nation, protests for civil rights, and against the war, were rampant, and the trust between the American people and their government was eroding. As Nixon faced re-election in 1972, he was determined to win by a wide margin, solidifying his mandate and power.

However, Nixon's political paranoia had grown significantly during his presidency. He saw enemies everywhere – particularly in the press, which he believed was out to destroy him. This paranoia influenced his actions, leading to unethical decisions driven by fear rather than strategy. Nixon's belief that his opponents were conspiring against him laid the groundwork for his eventual undoing.

Sowing the Seeds of Mistake

The seeds of Nixon's fall were sown during his 1972 re-election campaign, when his team, known as the Committee to Re-Elect the President (CREEP), became involved in a series of illegal activities. The most infamous of these was the break-in at the Democratic National Committee headquarters at the Watergate complex.

Nixon's campaign sought to gain an advantage by spying on his political rivals, but when the burglars were caught, it set off a chain of events that would forever alter American politics.

The real scandal wasn't just the break-in – it was the cover-up. Nixon believed he could manipulate the system to keep his presidency intact. Instead of admitting wrongdoing, he doubled down, directing the FBI to halt its investigation, and paying hush money to the burglars. These actions turned a manageable crisis into a national scandal.

Have you ever tried to cover up a mistake, only to find the situation spiralling out of control? What might have happened if you'd admitted fault early on?

Reaping What Was Sown

As the Watergate investigation deepened, it became clear that the cover-up led directly to the Oval Office. Journalists Bob Woodward and Carl Bernstein, aided by a secret informant known as Deep Throat, exposed a web of corruption. But the final blow came with the release of the Nixon tapes – recordings that revealed Nixon's direct involvement in obstructing justice.

The tapes were undeniable proof of Nixon's misconduct. His credibility with Congress and the American public crumbled. Facing impeachment, Nixon resigned on August 8, 1974, becoming the first U.S. president to do so. His fall from grace was swift and complete, overshadowing his once-promising legacy.

Nixon's need for control cost him everything.

Are there areas in your life where fear of losing control is leading you to make poor decisions? What would happen if you let go of that fear and chose integrity instead?

Harvesting the Lessons

Richard Nixon's downfall serves as a powerful reminder of the dangers of paranoia, mistrust, and the belief that power places someone above accountability. His presidency unravelled not because of the original crime but because of his decision to cover it up and abuse his authority.

RICHARD NIXON – THE SCANDAL THAT SHOOK THE NATION

These lessons are as relevant today as they were during Nixon's time. Unchecked fear and the desire to maintain control can drive anyone – from world leaders to everyday individuals – toward poor decisions. Nixon's story shows that the willingness to admit fault and take responsibility, though difficult, can often prevent a crisis from escalating.

Here are three scenarios to reflect on, with reflections to help apply these lessons to your own life:

Scenario 1: Fear of Failure

You're invited to present an idea at work, but you're worried about stumbling over your words or being judged. You feel tempted to decline, telling yourself that someone else would do a better job.

Reflection Questions:

- What's the real source of this fear – lack of preparation, self-doubt, or past experiences?

- If fear wasn't a factor, how would you approach this opportunity?

- What small step could help you build confidence, like rehearsing, or asking for support?

Scenario 2: Deflecting Mistakes

During a group project, you realise a mistake you made has caused delays. Instead of acknowledging it, you shift the blame to unclear instructions, or someone else's input.

Reflection Questions:

- How does avoiding responsibility make you feel in the short term? How about in the long term?

- What might change if you admitted the mistake and offered a solution?

- How could taking responsibility build trust with your team or peers?

Scenario 3: Struggling with Control

You're planning a family vacation and feel the need to make every decision, from the itinerary to the restaurant reservations. When others suggest ideas, you feel frustrated, thinking their choices might ruin the experience.

Reflection Questions:

- What's behind your need for control – fear of failure, a desire to protect others, or something else?

- How might delegating decisions strengthen your relationships and ease your stress?

- What could trusting others teach you about collaboration or flexibility?

Final Note

These scenarios highlight common ways fear and control show up in everyday life. As you reflect, consider: Where in your life are fear or control holding you back? What would change if you leaned into openness and trust instead?

Tilling the Soil of Reflection

Nixon's story challenges us to think about how we handle power, mistakes, and fear. Are we willing to confront our fears openly, admit our mistakes, and stay true to our values? Or do we fall into the trap of secrecy and control, believing that we can manipulate our way out of trouble?

When faced with a challenge, do you Prioritise integrity and trust – or short-term wins that may come at a greater cost? Nixon's story reminds us that true leadership isn't about avoiding failure, but about how we handle it when it comes.

Breaking New Ground

Picture a dam holding back a vast reservoir of water. It's a powerful structure, built to channel and control immense forces. But when small cracks form, and those cracks are ignored, the pressure builds until the dam finally bursts – causing devastation downstream. Richard Nixon's presidency is like that dam: a structure built on ambition and political acumen, but ultimately undermined by unchecked dishonesty and a refusal to address the cracks in his integrity.

Nixon rose to incredible heights, navigating a complex political landscape with skill and intelligence. Yet, the Watergate scandal exposed the cracks in his foundation: secrecy; paranoia; and a willingness to bend the rules to protect himself. Like water seeping through a dam, his actions eroded the trust of the American people and his allies, leading to his historic resignation.

Have you ever tried to ignore small "cracks" in your own life – ethical shortcuts, unspoken conflicts, or decisions made out of fear? What would happen if you addressed them before the pressure builds? Nixon's story challenges us to examine the cracks in our own integrity before they become too large to contain.

Cultivating Growth

Richard Nixon's story is a stark reminder of how even small lapses in integrity can snowball into catastrophic consequences. His downfall wasn't the result of a single action, but a series of choices that compromised his values and eroded the trust he worked so hard to build.

Key Takeaways

- **Integrity Is the Foundation**: Just as a dam relies on its structural integrity, your character relies on honesty and accountability. Even small lapses can lead to major consequences.
- **Transparency Builds Trust**: Trust isn't a given – it's earned through consistent transparency and ethical behaviour. When mistakes happen, owning up to them strengthens relationships and credibility.
- **Address Cracks Early**: Problems ignored today become crises tomorrow. Confronting issues early, no matter how small, prevents them from escalating out of control.

True growth begins with the courage to confront your own cracks – those small compromises, fears, or lapses in judgment that might seem harmless but can grow over time. Nixon's legacy shows us the cost of ignoring them.

By addressing issues early, being honest with yourself and others, and choosing integrity over expediency, you can avoid the kind of collapse that comes when trust is lost.

So, here's your challenge: What cracks exist in your own dam? Are there areas where you've bent the truth, ignored accountability, or let fear dictate your decisions? How can you address them now to prevent future damage?

Growth doesn't mean being perfect. It means being honest about your flaws and committed to repairing them before the pressure becomes too great to bear.

PLANTING STAGE 4

Diego Maradona – The Brilliance and the Downfall

Quote: "I made mistakes, and I paid for them"
– Diego Maradona

Image: Diego Maradona holding the FIFA World Cup trophy, 1986. Public domain via Wikimedia Commons.

DIEGO MARADONA – THE BRILLIANCE AND THE DOWNFALL

Before You Read:

If you've ever seen someone's talent outpace their discipline—or felt that tension yourself—Maradona's story will hit home. He shares some DNA with Steve Jobs (Chapter 8), though their outcomes differ. Or look at King Ludwig II (Chapter 5), another gifted dreamer whose world slowly slipped out of reach.

Breaking Ground: The Rise of Diego Maradona

Diego Maradona was more than a footballer – he was a legend. Born in 1960 in Villa Fiorito, a poor neighbourhood outside Buenos Aires, Maradona rose from extreme poverty to become one of the greatest players the world has ever seen.

A football prodigy, he was celebrated for his unmatched ball control, agility, and ability to mesmerise defenders with his footwork.

At just 16, Maradona made his debut for Argentina's national team, marking the beginning of a journey to global stardom. His dazzling performance in the 1986 FIFA World Cup, where he almost single-handedly led Argentina to victory, cemented his status as one of the sport's all-time greats.

The "Hand of God" goal, followed by the "Goal of the Century", showcased his genius – bold, creative, and unstoppable.

Off the field, Maradona became a symbol of hope and pride, particularly for Argentina and Naples, where he led Napoli to unprecedented success. His story was one of triumph over adversity, bringing joy to millions. Yet behind the brilliance, personal struggles began to emerge, ultimately tarnishing his legacy.

The Ground from Which It Grew: Fame and Pressure

With fame came overwhelming pressure. By the time Maradona joined Napoli in 1984, he was already a global superstar. His arrival transformed Napoli, leading the team to its first Serie A titles in 1987 and 1990. In Naples, Maradona was worshipped as a saviour, a beacon of hope for the city's people.

However, such adoration came with enormous expectations. Maradona was expected to shoulder the weight of the club, the nation, and his own reputation. To cope with the unrelenting demands, he turned to unhealthy escapes.

The constant pressures of fame and fortune began to take their toll, and Maradona's involvement with questionable figures in Naples led to a downward spiral into drug addiction.

The intoxicating mix of success and the pressures of fame fuelled Maradona's reckless behaviour off the pitch. While he continued to produce magical moments on the field, the cracks in his personal life became increasingly visible.

Sowing the Seeds of Mistake

Maradona's greatest mistake was believing that his immense talent could shield him from the consequences of his actions. His genius on the field allowed him to overlook erratic behaviour and indulgent habits for years, but personal demons – particularly his addiction to drugs – began to erode both his health and his career.

By the late 1980s, Maradona's cocaine addiction was widely known within football circles, though it was often ignored or concealed due to his importance to Napoli and Argentina. His ties to the criminal underworld in Naples only exacerbated his struggles. He began missing training sessions, alienating teammates, and gaining notoriety for his off-field exploits.

In 1991, Maradona's lifestyle caught up with him when he tested positive for cocaine, resulting in a 15-month ban from football. This suspension marked the beginning of his public downfall. The football icon who had once stood atop the world now found himself embroiled in scandal and disgrace.

Despite his eventual return to football, Maradona's battles with addiction persisted. His brilliance on the pitch was undeniable, but his failure to confront his personal struggles ultimately limited his ability to reclaim the greatness that had once defined his career.

Reaping What Was Sown

The consequences of Maradona's choices were devastating. His addiction to drugs, combined with his excessive lifestyle, took a severe toll on his health and career. In 1994, after briefly returning to international football, Maradona was once again suspended, this time for testing positive for a banned substance, ephedrine, during the World Cup. It was another public humiliation for a man who had once been at the pinnacle of the sport.

Off the pitch, Maradona's personal life was plagued by legal battles, paternity suits, and financial struggles. His relationships with family and former teammates became strained, and his erratic behaviour made headlines. The fame that had once elevated him now entrapped him, and Maradona found himself caught in a cycle of addiction and self-destruction.

As Maradona aged, his health deteriorated rapidly. He struggled with obesity, underwent multiple surgeries, and suffered from heart and liver issues. Despite several attempts at rehabilitation and recovery, Maradona never fully overcame his demons.

In 2020, at the age of 60, Maradona passed away from a heart attack, leaving behind a complicated legacy. Fans mourned the loss of a football genius, yet many also reflected on the tragedy of his life – a man whose extraordinary talent was ultimately undone by the personal struggles he could not conquer.

Harvesting the Lessons

Diego Maradona's rise and fall highlight the dangers of unchecked fame, poor choices, and the failure to Prioritise personal well-being. While his extraordinary talent made him one of the greatest footballers in history, his struggles with addiction, scandals, and health issues, overshadowed his achievements and ultimately shortened his career.

Maradona's story is a powerful reminder that success on the surface does not always equate to true fulfillment or stability. It shows how neglecting self-discipline and failing to address personal struggles can lead even the most talented individuals down a path of self-destruction.

The lessons of Maradona's life resonate deeply today, especially in a world that often idolises public figures while ignoring the pressures they face. His story reminds us of the importance of self-awareness, seeking help when needed, and balancing ambition with personal care to achieve lasting success and happiness.

Here are three scenarios to reflect on, with reflections to help apply these lessons to your own life:

Scenario 1: Relying on Success to Excuse Poor Behaviour

You've recently achieved a major milestone in your career, receiving accolades for your work. While celebrating, you notice yourself cutting corners in other areas – missing deadlines, showing up late, or neglecting commitments – justifying it because of your success.

Reflection Questions:

- Are there areas in your life where you're allowing success to overshadow accountability?

- How might this mindset impact your relationships, work, or personal growth in the long run?

- What actions could help you stay grounded and aligned with your values?

Scenario 2: Ignoring Signs of a Destructive Habit

You've started relying on a particular coping mechanism to manage stress, like binge-watching TV, or excessive scrolling on social media. It helps temporarily, but it's starting to interfere with your daily goals, leaving you less productive and more frustrated.

Reflection Questions:

- Are there habits or behaviours in your life that might be hindering your growth?

- What early signs might you be ignoring, and how can you address them before they escalate?

- What small, actionable steps could you take to replace this habit with a healthier coping mechanism?

Scenario 3: Neglecting Self-Care Amid Success

You're working hard toward a promotion, putting in long hours and skipping meals or workouts. While the effort feels worthwhile, you've noticed increased fatigue, irritability, and less connection with loved ones.

Reflection Questions:

- Are your current efforts sustainable, or are they compromising your well-being?

- How might better self-care improve your focus, energy, and relationships?

- What adjustments could you make to create a balance between your goals and your health?

Final Reflection

Maradona's story reminds us that talent alone isn't enough to sustain greatness – it must be paired with accountability, self-awareness, and self-care. As you reflect, ask yourself:

- Are you addressing the deeper causes of your challenges, or relying on temporary solutions?
- How might prioritising your well-being help you achieve long-term success and fulfillment?

Tilling the Soil of Reflection

Maradona's story is a reminder that talent and success can only take us so far. True growth comes from addressing our challenges head-on, not avoiding them.

When faced with pressure, what do you lean on? Do you focus on long-term solutions, or are you drawn to quick fixes? Reflecting on these questions can help you make healthier, more sustainable choices in your own life.

Breaking New Ground

Imagine a seedling planted in rich soil – it has all the potential to grow into a towering tree. But what happens if the roots don't go deep enough? Without a strong foundation, even the most promising growth can falter when storms come. Diego Maradona's life is a story of incredible talent, raw passion, and ultimate collapse – a seedling with limitless potential but shallow roots.

Maradona's rise to soccer greatness was meteoric. His skill was unparalleled, his charisma undeniable, and his connection with fans unmatched. Yet, beneath the brilliance, cracks were forming.

His struggles with addiction, lack of discipline, and inability to cope with fame became storms that uprooted his legacy. Despite his achievements, Maradona's story is as much about missed opportunities for personal growth as it is about athletic triumphs.

Now, think about your own life. Are there areas where your talents or successes might be outpacing your personal growth? Are you cultivating deep roots – strong values, discipline, and balance – that can weather life's challenges? Maradona's story asks us to reflect on what it takes to turn potential into sustainable success.

Cultivating Growth

Diego Maradona's life is a powerful lesson in how unaddressed personal struggles can undermine even the greatest talent. His story reminds us that success isn't just about what you achieve – it's about how you sustain it and the legacy you leave behind.

Key Takeaways:

- **Talent Needs Discipline**: Natural ability can take you far, but without discipline and hard work, it's easy to lose focus and falter under pressure.
- **Balance Is Crucial**. Fame, success, or any form of recognition can be overwhelming. Prioritising mental health, relationships, and self-awareness creates stability.
- **Build A Strong Foundation**: Success should rest on values and habits that keep you grounded. Without deep roots, the storms of life can uproot even the most promising future.

True growth means going beyond raw talent or external success to build a life that can stand the test of time. Maradona's legacy teaches us that brilliance alone isn't enough – it must be paired with self-awareness, discipline, and balance to create something enduring.

So, here's your challenge: Are there areas where your personal growth hasn't kept pace with your achievements? Are you cultivating strong roots to sustain your success, or are you relying solely on your talent to carry you through?

Growth isn't about perfection; it's about planting your roots deeper every day. Build habits that nurture your mind, body, and spirit, so that when life's storms come, you'll have the strength to stand tall and thrive.

PLANTING STAGE 5

King Ludwig II of Bavaria – The Dreamer's Downfall

Quote: "I wish to remain an eternal enigma to myself and others"
– King Ludwig II of Bavaria

Image: King Ludwig II of Bavaria, 1865. Public domain via Wikimedia Commons.

KING LUDWIG II OF BAVARIA – THE DREAMER'S DOWNFALL

Before You Read:

Do you retreat into your work when the world gets overwhelming? King Ludwig built literal castles to escape reality. He shares a surprising kinship with Alfred Nobel (Chapter 15), who also tried to reshape his legacy—but with vastly different results. Or look back at Maradona (Chapter 4), whose brilliance also came with a cost.

Breaking Ground: The Dreaming King

King Ludwig II of Bavaria, often called the "Fairy Tale King", is remembered for his artistic vision, passion for grand architecture, and the iconic castles he built, including the world-famous Neuschwanstein Castle.

Born in 1845, Ludwig ascended to the throne at just 18. From the beginning, he sought to create a kingdom that embodied beauty, splendour, and fantasy – an ideal world far removed from the political strife of his time.

Ludwig was a highly introverted and eccentric ruler, drawn more to poets, musicians, and artists than to politicians or military leaders. He idolised the composer Richard Wagner and envisioned a kingdom where art and culture reigned supreme. His castles were physical manifestations of his dream, combining medieval and Gothic inspirations with his personal fantasies.

But Ludwig's dream came at a heavy cost. His obsession with constructing extravagant castles drained the Bavarian treasury, and his detachment from political realities alienated him from his government. Ultimately, his refusal to balance artistic ambition with practical governance contributed to his tragic downfall.

The Ground from Which It Grew: A Kingdom on The Brink

When Ludwig II became king in 1864, Bavaria was a small kingdom in a fractured Germany. The political landscape was turbulent, as Otto von Bismarck worked to unify the German states under Prussian rule.

Ludwig, however, showed little interest in political manoeuvring or governance. Instead, he retreated into his world of art, beauty, and imagination, leaving much of the ruling to his ministers.

While Bavaria struggled politically and economically, Ludwig focused on building his dream castles – Neuschwanstein, Linderhof, and Herrenchiemsee. These projects were not practical fortresses, but elaborate personal monuments to his romantic vision of a medieval kingdom. The castles, though magnificent, placed an immense financial strain on the Bavarian treasury.

As Bavaria faltered, Ludwig remained fixated on his dreams, steadfastly believing their value outweighed any cost. His ministers, increasingly concerned by his lack of engagement and financial mismanagement, struggled to gain his attention.

How do you ensure that your focus on what inspires you doesn't overshadow what sustains you?

Sowing the Seeds of Mistake

Ludwig's greatest mistake was his obsession with building castles at the expense of his kingdom's financial stability. He spared no expense in constructing his architectural masterpieces.

Neuschwanstein, for example, was a fairy-tale castle brought to life, complete with soaring towers and elaborate interiors – but it was also a financial disaster. Each new project pushed Bavaria deeper into debt, yet Ludwig continued spending as if the resources were infinite.

Rather than addressing the kingdom's growing debt or engaging with the political realities of his time, Ludwig withdrew further into his fantasy world. He refused to heed the warnings of his advisors, isolating himself from those who could have helped him manage the crisis. His castles became both a refuge from reality and the seeds of his downfall.

By 1885, Ludwig's financial situation was dire. He had borrowed heavily from foreign banks to fund his projects, leaving Bavaria in financial disarray. His ministers, unable to curtail his spending or gain his cooperation, decided drastic action was necessary.

Have you ever pursued something so intently that you missed the signs telling you to stop and reassess?

Reaping What Was Sown

The consequences of Ludwig's actions were inevitable. In 1886, his ministers declared him mentally unfit to rule, citing his increasingly erratic behaviour and extravagant spending.

A commission of doctors – none of whom had personally examined him – deemed him insane. Ludwig was deposed and placed under arrest at Neuschwanstein Castle, the very symbol of his dreams and his downfall.

Shortly after, Ludwig was moved to Berg Castle near Lake Starnberg. Days later, he was found dead in the lake alongside his psychiatrist under mysterious circumstances. To this day, whether his death was a suicide, or the result of foul play remains uncertain.

While Ludwig's castles have since become beloved cultural landmarks and tourist attractions, during his lifetime they were seen as monuments to reckless ambition. His inability to balance his grand dreams with practical responsibilities led to his removal from power, and left Bavaria grappling with the financial consequences of his decisions.

What legacy are you building, and is it one that balances your dreams with the reality of what's needed to sustain them?

Harvesting the Lessons

King Ludwig II of Bavaria's life illustrates the risks of retreating into fantasy and ignoring the practical responsibilities of leadership. Known as the "Fairy Tale King", Ludwig poured immense resources into building extravagant castles, including Neuschwanstein, while neglecting the financial and political realities of his kingdom. His obsession with grandeur and isolation ultimately led to his deposition and mysterious death.

Ludwig's story serves as a reminder that dreams and creativity, while vital, must be balanced with responsibility and realism. Neglecting the needs of others or the larger picture can alienate allies and weaken even the most inspired visions.

Ludwig's legacy teaches us the importance of grounding ambition in practicality, and to consider how our choices impact those around us. His castles may stand as symbols of wonder, but his reign reflects the consequences of failing to connect imagination with the demands of reality.

Here are three scenarios to reflect on, with reflections to help apply these lessons to your own life:

KING LUDWIG II OF BAVARIA – THE DREAMER'S DOWNFALL

Scenario 1: Pursuing Ambitions Without Considering Costs

You're working on a passion project that excites you, but it's demanding more time, money, or energy, than you initially anticipated. You've started to notice its impact on your finances or relationships, yet you feel reluctant to scale back or reassess.

Reflection Questions:

- Are you accounting for the broader costs of pursuing your goals?

- How might your choices today impact your well-being or relationships in the future?

- What small adjustments could make your efforts more sustainable?

Scenario 2: Avoiding Responsibilities While Focusing on Passions

You've been spending extra time on a hobby or interest and, while it's fulfilling, other areas of your life – like work deadlines, bills, or family commitments – are being neglected. You sense the growing tension, but haven't addressed it directly.

Reflection Questions:

- Are there responsibilities you've been avoiding because of your focus on personal interests?

- How might addressing those neglected areas improve your sense of balance or reduce stress?

- What's one step you could take to realign your focus without abandoning your passion?

KING LUDWIG II OF BAVARIA – THE DREAMER'S DOWNFALL

Scenario 3: Isolating Yourself from Feedback

You're pursuing a goal and feel so strongly about your vision that you've stopped asking for input from others. When someone offers constructive feedback, you dismiss it, believing they don't understand or share your passion.

Reflection Questions:

- How might pride or discomfort be preventing you from seeking valuable guidance?

- Who in your life could provide perspective to help you refine your vision or avoid pitfalls?

- What would happen if you sought out feedback and considered it with an open mind?

Final Reflection

As you reflect on these scenarios, consider:

- Are your ambitions building something sustainable and beneficial, or are they creating unintended strain?
- What balance can you strike between pursuing your dreams and fulfilling your responsibilities?

Tilling the Soil of Reflection

King Ludwig II's story challenges us to think about the balance between our dreams and responsibilities. His castles, while breathtaking, came at the expense of his kingdom's stability, and his own downfall. Ludwig's story reminds us that unchecked ambition can lead to unintended consequences. The beauty we create in our lives must be built on a foundation of foresight and balance.

Are your ambitions balanced with practical responsibilities, or are you sacrificing stability in pursuit of a dream? Are you confronting the realities of your situation, or retreating into fantasy to avoid them?

Breaking New Ground

Imagine a gardener who creates the most awe-inspiring garden anyone has ever seen – every flower perfectly arranged, every pathway a work of art. Visitors marvel at its beauty, unaware that just beyond the garden lies the gardener's own house, neglected and crumbling into ruin.

King Ludwig II of Bavaria's life mirrors this image: a man so consumed by his grand visions of beauty and creativity that he neglected the foundations of his own reality.

Ludwig poured his heart and soul into his castles, turning dreams into breathtaking architectural wonders. Yet, while his creations thrived, his kingdom's finances, his relationships, and even his sense of self, slowly fell apart. His obsession with perfection and escapism came at a high cost, isolating him and ultimately contributing to his tragic downfall.

Have you ever become so focused on one goal or project that other important areas of your life were left to deteriorate? Ludwig's story invites us to ask: Are you tending to your own "house", or are you neglecting it in favour of building something impressive for others to admire?

Cultivating Growth

King Ludwig II's life is a powerful metaphor for the risks of pouring energy into external achievements while ignoring the internal structures that support them. His castles endure as symbols of ambition, but his life reminds us of the importance of balance and self-care.

Key Takeaways

- **Build Your Foundation First**: Before focusing on outward achievements, make sure your inner world – your relationships, mental health, and responsibilities – is strong and stable.
- **Beware of Escapism**: Dreams and passions are vital, but they shouldn't be an escape from the realities of life. Balance creativity with practicality.
- **Nurture What Matters Most**: Like the gardener's house, your personal life requires care and attention. Neglecting it for the sake of outward success can lead to collapse.

True growth comes from balancing the pursuit of dreams with the maintenance of your personal foundation. Ludwig's story reminds us that, while creating beauty is admirable, it must never come at the expense of our well-being, relationships, or responsibilities.

So, here's your challenge: Are there areas in your life where you've been tending to the "garden" while neglecting your "house"? How can you begin to rebuild and care for the foundation that supports everything else?

Growth isn't just about building something impressive for the world to see – it's about ensuring that what lies behind the scenes is just as strong, resilient, and beautiful. Dream boldly, but don't forget to take care of your own house.

PART 2
SETBACKS – LESSONS IN RECOVERY AND RESILIENCE

In every story of success, there are moments where ambition and action collide with unforeseen consequences. For some, these missteps leave scars, but not destruction. Their mistakes, while significant, don't lead to complete ruin. Instead, they result in setbacks – challenges that hinder progress or tarnish reputations without erasing achievements entirely.

In this section, we delve into the lives of five figures whose errors carried lasting consequences, shaping their legacies in profound ways. These individuals achieved remarkable success, but their decisions – whether driven by overconfidence, resistance to change, or a lack of foresight – left undeniable marks on their careers and lives.

From Elon Musk's erratic behaviour to the Empress Dowager Cixi's resistance to modernisation, these stories show how even those with extraordinary vision and talent can stumble when balance is lost.

These figures remind us that setbacks don't always mean destruction, but they do often carry a cost:

- **Elon Musk, the visionary entrepreneur,** whose habit of over-promising, and unpredictable actions, created challenges for his companies and public trust.
- **Mark Zuckerberg, the social media pioneer,** whose handling of user data during the Cambridge Analytica scandal raised questions about privacy and ethics in the digital age.
- **Steve Jobs, the creative genius,** whose inability to collaborate initially led to his ousting from Apple before he returned to reshape the company's legacy.
- **Empress Dowager Cixi, the powerful ruler,** who resisted modernisation during a critical period, leaving China vulnerable to foreign powers.
- **Marie Curie, the trailblazing scientist,** whose unwavering dedication to her work came at a great personal cost to her health.

Before you begin, think of a time when you faced a setback that carried unexpected consequences. How might a different approach have altered the outcome? Let these stories inspire you to reflect on your own path, and consider how even small adjustments can steer you toward resilience and growth.

These setbacks reveal that success alone is not enough to guarantee sustainability. They serve as reminders of the importance of foresight, accountability, and adaptability, in achieving and maintaining greatness. What are you doing today to ensure your own success doesn't come at an avoidable cost?

PLANTING STAGE 6

Elon Musk – The Visionary Who Overpromised

Quote: "When something is important enough, you do it even if the odds are not in your favour"
– Elon Musk

Image: Elon Musk (2018) by Debbie Rowe. Licensed under CC BY-SA 3.0 via Wikimedia Commons.

Before You Read:

Musk is a lightning rod: inspiring, frustrating, unpredictable. If you're interested in the risk/reward of public leadership, compare him to Napoleon (Chapter 2)—both shot for the stars, literally or figuratively, and faced consequences when overreach caught up. Or jump to Empress Cixi (Chapter 9), who resisted change rather than chased it.

Breaking Ground: The Visionary Leader

Elon Musk, born in South Africa in 1971, is one of the most influential entrepreneurs of our time. His companies – Tesla, SpaceX, Neuralink, and The Boring Company – are pushing the boundaries of what is possible in transportation, space exploration, and renewable energy.

Musk's bold vision to revolutionise industries, and create a future that defies the limitations of the present, has inspired millions and reshaped global technology.

However, Musk's meteoric rise has not been without controversy. His eccentric behaviour, particularly on social media, combined with his tendency to overpromise, has led to significant challenges for both him and his companies.

Despite these setbacks, Musk's resilience and unrelenting ambition have kept him at the forefront of innovation. His journey is a prime example of a "setback", where mistakes are meaningful but not career-ending.

The Ground from Which It Grew: Ambition and Public Scrutiny

Musk's relentless pursuit of transformative ideas has been the foundation of his rise to fame. From launching Tesla, which revolutionised the electric vehicle industry, to founding SpaceX with the audacious goal of making life multi-planetary, Musk has consistently set his sights on objectives that many deemed unattainable.

But Musk's bold ambitions have come with heightened public scrutiny, especially as he adopted an unconventional leadership style. His use of social media, particularly Twitter (now X), has both amplified his personal brand and created significant PR and legal problems for his companies.

While his visionary approach attracts followers, it has also led to volatility and controversy, exemplifying the fine line Musk walks between brilliance and recklessness.

Are there areas in your life where bold ambition might be creating unnecessary challenges?

Sowing the Seeds of Mistake

One of Musk's most publicised missteps occurred in 2018 when he tweeted that he was considering taking Tesla private at $420 per share, and that funding had been secured. This statement caused Tesla's stock to fluctuate wildly and led to an investigation by the U.S. Securities and Exchange Commission (SEC). It quickly became clear that the tweet was premature and misleading, leading to Musk being fined $20 million and stepping down as Tesla's chairman, though he retained his CEO role.

This incident revealed Musk's tendency to overpromise and act impulsively, especially on platforms like Twitter, where his statements could have immediate financial repercussions.

Musk's habit of setting overly ambitious timelines has also frustrated investors and customers. For example, his repeated predictions that Tesla would deliver fully autonomous cars, sooner than feasible, have created gaps between his promises and reality.

Adding to this, Musk's erratic public behaviour – such as smoking marijuana during a 2018 appearance on *The Joe Rogan Experience* – raised concerns about his judgment. While Musk continues to innovate, these public missteps have strained his credibility and caused temporary financial setbacks for his companies.

How might impulsive actions in your own life be creating avoidable challenges or setbacks?

Reaping What Was Sown

The consequences of Musk's mistakes have been significant, but not catastrophic. The SEC lawsuit, the fluctuations in Tesla's stock, and the criticism of his erratic behaviour, have led to increased scrutiny from investors and regulators. Tesla's stock volatility, in particular, has made the company subject to dramatic financial swings, creating uncertainty for its future.

Yet, Musk has proven incredibly resilient. Despite these controversies, Tesla has grown into one of the world's most valuable companies, and SpaceX has achieved incredible milestones, including sending astronauts to the International Space Station.

Musk's ability to recover from his missteps, and continue innovating, shows that while bold visionaries may stumble, they are not easily derailed.

Musk's story serves as a reminder that ambition, when unrestrained by caution and thoughtful execution, can create long-term challenges. While his reputation as a visionary endures, the public controversies and legal consequences have cast a shadow over his legacy.

What steps can you take today to ensure that your boldest ambitions are supported by thoughtful planning and execution?

Harvesting the Lessons

Elon Musk's career, while marked by incredible innovation, also demonstrates the challenges of overextending oneself, and the risks of impulsive decision-making. From production delays at Tesla, to controversial tweets that have caused market disruptions and legal troubles, Musk's missteps show the fine line between visionary leadership and reckless behaviour.

Musk's story highlights the importance of managing bold ambition with careful execution and communication. While his ability to dream big has revolutionised industries, his challenges reveal the need for discipline, focus, and an awareness of the broader impact of one's actions.

The lessons from Musk's successes and struggles remind us that, while ambition is essential for growth, thoughtful planning, consistent effort, and accountability are equally critical to achieving sustainable success. His story encourages us to balance creativity with responsibility in our own pursuits.

Here are three scenarios to reflect on, with reflections to help apply these lessons to your own life:

Scenario 1: Setting Realistic Goals Without Overpromising

You've taken on a big project, and set an ambitious deadline to impress your team or client. As the deadline approaches, you realise the timeline wasn't realistic, and frustration begins to build – both for you and others involved.

Reflection Questions:

- Are your current goals realistic, or are they driven by the desire to prove something?

- How could setting achievable milestones build trust and credibility with those relying on you?

- What adjustments could make your goals ambitious yet manageable?

Scenario 2: Thinking Before You Communicate

You're preparing to send an email, or post something on social media, in the heat of the moment, expressing frustration or making a bold statement. Later, you wonder if it might have been wiser to pause and reflect before hitting send.

Reflection Questions:

- How often do you consider the impact of your words before sharing them?

- What's one way pausing before speaking or writing could improve clarity or avoid misunderstandings?

- How might consulting a trusted colleague or friend before communicating help you refine your message?

Scenario 3: Recovering From Mistakes

You recently made an error in a leadership or professional role that had visible consequences, leaving you feeling embarrassed or frustrated. While you've apologised, you still find it hard to move forward confidently.

Reflection Questions:

- How do you usually respond to mistakes – by learning from them, or by letting them undermine your confidence?

- What steps can you take to turn this setback into an opportunity for growth?

- How could owning your mistake demonstrate accountability and strengthen your reputation?

Final Reflection

Musk's story reminds us that success isn't just about big ideas – it's about balancing ambition with practicality, communicating thoughtfully, and growing from failures. Ask yourself:

- Are your actions building trust and credibility with those around you?
- How might pausing, reassessing, and adapting, help you achieve lasting success?

Tilling the Soil of Reflection

Elon Musk's career illustrates the fine line between visionary ambition and reckless overreach. His story challenges us to think about the balance between bold goals and grounded execution.

Are you setting expectations that inspire but remain achievable? Are your words and actions aligned with the leader you want to be? How do you recover from mistakes and learn to build resilience for the future?

Breaking New Ground

Imagine planting seeds in a fertile field. The seeds hold incredible potential but, if they're sown hastily or without care, they can sprout weeds that choke the growth of everything around them.

Elon Musk's missteps, like his infamous 2018 tweet about taking Tesla private, are like those hastily planted seeds – decisions made impulsively that sprouted unintended consequences, requiring significant time and resources to repair the damage.

While Musk's vision has propelled industries forward, his tendency to act on impulse, particularly on public platforms like Twitter, has caused ripple effects – fluctuating stock prices, regulatory investigations, and damage to his credibility.

Just as a farmer must carefully plan where and how to sow seeds to ensure healthy crops, Musk's story teaches us the importance of considering the broader impact of our actions before rushing forward.

Have you ever acted impulsively, only to find yourself dealing with unintended consequences? Musk's story challenges us to reflect on how we can temper passion and ambition with forethought and discipline.

Cultivating Growth

Elon Musk's public missteps highlight the risks of acting on impulse and overpromising without a clear plan. His story invites us to consider how we can align bold ideas with thoughtful actions to avoid unnecessary setbacks.

Key Takeaways

- **Pause Before You Act**: Impulsive decisions, especially in high-stakes situations, can lead to unintended consequences. Take time to reflect before committing publicly.
- **Match Vision with Reality**: Ambition is vital, but setting unrealistic expectations can harm credibility and relationships. Strive for balance between vision and feasibility.
- **Control Your Narrative**: Public platforms amplify your words. Use them intentionally, knowing that your actions and statements have ripple effects beyond your immediate intentions.

True Growth

True growth lies in balancing ambition with caution. Musk's story reminds us that bold ideas need to be paired with thoughtful execution and disciplined communication. Acting without considering the broader consequences can derail even the best intentions.

So, here's your challenge: Are there areas in your life where impulsive actions or overpromising have caused setbacks? How can you slow down, reflect, and ensure your decisions align with your long-term goals?

Growth isn't about abandoning ambition – it's about channelling it wisely. Plan your actions like a careful farmer, sowing seeds deliberately and thoughtfully to ensure they produce the best possible harvest.

PLANTING STAGE 7

Mark Zuckerberg – The Man Who Connected the World and Exposed Its Privacy

Quote: "The question isn't 'What do we want to know about people?' It's 'What do people want to tell about themselves?'"
– Mark Zuckerberg

Image: Mark Zuckerberg (2014) by Presidencia de México. Licensed under CC BY 2.0 via Wikimedia Commons.

Before You Read:

If you're curious about what happens when quiet ambition meets global consequence, Zuckerberg's story offers a lesson in unintended damage. For another tale of trust gone sideways, revisit Nixon (Chapter 3). Or contrast him with Churchill (Chapter 13), who rebuilt trust through transparency and grit.

Breaking Ground: The Founder of Facebook

Mark Zuckerberg, one of the youngest billionaires in history, revolutionised how people communicate, share, and engage with the world through the creation of Facebook.

Born in 1984, Zuckerberg launched Facebook in 2004 while still a student at Harvard University. What began as a simple project to connect college students, quickly evolved into a global social media platform that would reshape communication on the Internet.

Facebook's success was unprecedented. It allowed people to connect with friends and family, join groups, and share content, with an ease and speed never seen before.

Under Zuckerberg's leadership, Facebook dominated the social media landscape, influencing politics, culture, and social interactions. Its algorithms personalised user experiences, curating news, ads, and connections that made Facebook a central part of daily life for billions of people.

However, Zuckerberg's remarkable success came with significant controversies, particularly around privacy and the ethical use of personal data. Facebook's rapid expansion was accompanied by growing scrutiny over how it managed user information, and a series of scandals would eventually taint Zuckerberg's legacy and create long-term challenges for the platform.

The Ground from Which It Grew: The Rise of Social Media

In the early 2000s, social media was still in its infancy. Platforms like Myspace and Friendster existed, but Facebook quickly outpaced them, thanks to its user-friendly design and rapid expansion.

What set Facebook apart was its ability to constantly evolve, turning into a sophisticated platform for advertisers, businesses, and individual users. Through data collection and targeted advertising, Facebook transformed into a powerful tool for marketers, giving businesses unprecedented access to audiences.

However, Facebook's data-driven model soon sparked concerns about privacy. As the company collected more personal information to tailor content and ads, questions arose about how this data was being used. The power of Facebook's algorithms to shape user experiences also led to concerns about its influence on public opinion, especially in the context of political advertising and fake news.

These concerns culminated in the Cambridge Analytica scandal, which would mark a turning point for Zuckerberg and Facebook.

How do the systems and routines you rely on shape the experiences of those around you? Are you prioritising ease and efficiency over ethical considerations?

Sowing the Seeds of Mistake

Zuckerberg's critical mistake was not in creating Facebook but in failing to anticipate the long-term consequences of the company's data practices.

In 2018, it was revealed that Cambridge Analytica, a political consulting firm, had accessed the personal data of millions of Facebook users without their consent. This data was used to influence voter behaviour in key political events, including the 2016 U.S. presidential election and the Brexit referendum.

The scandal exposed deep flaws in Facebook's privacy protections. Although the platform had policies in place, loopholes and lax enforcement allowed third parties to misuse personal data. Zuckerberg, who had always championed openness and connectivity, now faced global backlash over how Facebook managed its users' private information.

The fallout was swift. Zuckerberg was summoned to testify before U.S. Congress and the European Parliament, where he apologised for Facebook's role in the scandal and promised reforms. Despite these efforts, the damage was done – public trust in Facebook eroded, and Zuckerberg's leadership came under intense scrutiny. Many believed that Facebook had Prioritised growth and profits over user privacy and ethical responsibility.

The Cambridge Analytica scandal highlighted the dangers of failing to properly regulate a platform that had such immense power over personal data and public discourse. Zuckerberg's vision of connecting the world was overshadowed by revelations of how Facebook had been used for manipulation, misinformation, and breaches of trust.

When pursuing growth, are you fully considering the potential impact on others? How can you ensure your actions and systems are protecting those who rely on them?

Reaping What Was Sown

The consequences of Zuckerberg's oversight continue to affect Facebook and its reputation. The company has faced increased regulatory scrutiny worldwide, leading to calls for stronger privacy protections and greater accountability. In 2019, Facebook was fined $5 billion by the U.S. Federal Trade Commission (FTC) for its role in the Cambridge Analytica scandal – the largest penalty ever imposed on a tech company at the time.

Zuckerberg's personal reputation also suffered. Though he remains at the helm of Facebook (now rebranded as Meta), his image as a visionary leader was tarnished by the mishandling of privacy issues, and the platform's role in spreading misinformation.

MARK ZUCKERBERG – THE MAN WHO CONNECTED THE WORLD AND EXPOSED ITS PRIVACY

Critics argued that Zuckerberg had been too slow to address the core issues, and Facebook's continued controversies over data privacy and content moderation have left a lasting stain on his legacy.

While Facebook remains a dominant force in social media, the shadow of these scandals has changed how the public views the platform. What was once celebrated as a groundbreaking tool for connection is now seen by many as a cautionary tale about the ethical responsibilities of big tech.

When mistakes occur, are you willing to take swift and decisive action to rebuild trust? How can accountability become a cornerstone of your personal or professional leadership?

Harvesting the Lessons

Mark Zuckerberg's journey as the founder of Facebook reveals the dangers of prioritising growth over ethics and the importance of accountability in leadership.

From early controversies over user privacy, to the spread of misinformation on the platform, Zuckerberg's decisions often placed Facebook's success above the social and ethical consequences, leading to widespread criticism and global scrutiny.

Zuckerberg's story teaches us that progress without integrity can have lasting repercussions. While ambition and innovation can create extraordinary success, ignoring ethical concerns and the impact on others can erode trust and damage reputations.

The lessons from Zuckerberg's experiences remind us that true leadership requires balancing innovation with responsibility. His story challenges us to think critically about the long-term effects of our actions, ensuring that growth and impact align with values that foster trust and accountability.

Here are three scenarios to reflect on, with reflections to help apply these lessons to your own life:

Scenario 1: Considering the Consequences of Growth at All Costs

You're pursuing a goal – whether professional or personal – that requires rapid progress. While focused on achieving it, you notice signs of potential risks, such as strained relationships or overlooked details. Despite this, you feel compelled to push forward.

Reflection Questions:

- Are you considering the long-term consequences of prioritising growth over sustainability?

- How might pausing to assess risks strengthen your results and relationships?

- What steps can you take to balance progress with thoughtful planning?

Scenario 2: Being Transparent About Decisions

You're in a leadership role, and a recent decision has sparked questions from your team or loved ones. You realise you've avoided sharing the full reasoning behind your choice, fearing criticism or misunderstanding.

Reflection Questions:

- How does your level of transparency impact trust in your relationships or leadership?

- What's one way you could communicate your decisions more clearly and honestly?

- How might sharing your reasoning strengthen collaboration or understanding?

Scenario 3: Protecting Trust and Acting Ethically

Someone in your personal or professional circle relies on you for guidance or leadership. Recently, you've made decisions or actions that, while convenient for you, might have inadvertently strained their trust in your intentions.

Reflection Questions:

- What actions are you taking to protect the trust of those who depend on you?

- Are there areas where convenience or shortcuts have compromised the integrity of your decisions?

- How might small, intentional actions rebuild or reinforce trust in your relationships?

Final Reflection

Zuckerberg's story reminds us that growth and ambition must be tempered with ethics, transparency, and care for those who rely on us. As you reflect, consider:

- Are your actions aligned with your values and responsibilities?
- How might fostering trust and openness lead to stronger, more sustainable progress?

Tilling the Soil of Reflection

Mark Zuckerberg's story serves as a reminder that with great innovation comes great responsibility. Are there areas in your life where you are prioritising growth or success without considering the ethical implications? Are you transparent in your decisions, and do you take responsibility when mistakes are made?

How do you manage trust and responsibility in your life? Are your actions building confidence in others or creating potential risks that could harm relationships or your reputation?

Breaking New Ground

Picture a spider spinning a web. Each strand is meticulously crafted, forming a vast and intricate network designed to catch opportunities. But what happens when the spider becomes too focused on expanding the web, and neglects to monitor its strength or repair its weak points?

Mark Zuckerberg's story mirrors this image: a visionary who spun one of the most influential "webs" of the modern era – Facebook – but faced challenges when cracks in the design and execution of his creation began to show.

Zuckerberg's rapid expansion of Facebook revolutionised how we connect, but his focus on growth and innovation often came at the expense of addressing deeper issues, such as privacy concerns, misinformation, and ethical responsibility.

Like a spider that overextends its web, he faced moments where the very foundation of his creation was threatened, shaking public trust and sparking global scrutiny.

Have you ever been so focused on growing or expanding an idea that you overlooked its structural weaknesses? Zuckerberg's story invites us to reflect: Are we building something sustainable, or are we stretching ourselves too thin, risking the integrity of our "web"?

Cultivating Growth

Mark Zuckerberg's story is a lesson in the importance of balancing growth with responsibility. While innovation can drive remarkable success, it must be paired with vigilance to ensure long-term stability and trust.

Key Takeaways:

- **Tend to the Web**: Growth is important, but regular checks and repairs are essential to ensure the integrity of your foundation. Ignoring weak points can lead to collapse.
- **Balance Growth with Responsibility**: Ambition should be tempered by ethical considerations and accountability to those affected by your decisions.
- **Learn from Challenges**: Mistakes and setbacks are opportunities to strengthen your "web". Use them to address weaknesses and build greater resilience.

True growth lies in maintaining the balance between innovation and responsibility. Zuckerberg's story teaches us that while creating something vast and influential is admirable, it's equally important to ensure that it is ethical, sustainable, and serves the greater good.

So, here's your challenge: Are there areas in your life where you're focused on expanding your "web" but neglecting to strengthen its foundation? How can you slow down to address vulnerabilities and ensure that what you're building is sustainable?

Growth isn't just about creating the biggest web – it's about crafting one strong enough to withstand the storms of life. Be like the spider who not only builds but also strengthens and repairs, ensuring the web endures and fulfills its purpose.

PLANTING STAGE 8

Steve Jobs – The Visionary's Fall and Return

Quote: "Sometimes life is going to hit you in the head with a brick. Don't lose faith."
– Steve Jobs

Image: Steve Jobs (2010) by MetalGearLiquid, based on a photo by Matt Yohe. Licensed under CC BY-SA 3.0 via Wikimedia Commons.

Before You Read:

Jobs was both a genius and a cautionary tale. If you've read Maradona (Chapter 4), you'll see how raw talent can become a liability. But unlike Maradona, Jobs learned to evolve—something Alfred Nobel (Chapter 15) also did when faced with the cost of his own creation.

Breaking Ground: The Visionary Leader

Steve Jobs was one of the most iconic and innovative figures of the modern age. Co-founding Apple Inc, he revolutionised industries from personal computing to mobile phones, music, and digital animation.

Born in 1955 in California, Jobs demonstrated an early knack for seeing possibilities where others saw limitations. Alongside Steve Wozniak, he built Apple into a technological powerhouse, launching groundbreaking products like the Apple II and the Macintosh, which transformed personal computing.

Jobs wasn't just a businessman; he was a creative genius driven by a relentless pursuit of excellence. His vision of integrating technology with intuitive, elegant design led to some of the most iconic innovations of the 20th and 21st centuries.

However, Jobs' leadership style was deeply flawed. His intense drive for perfection, and his abrasive, sometimes dismissive personality, created friction within Apple, ultimately leading to his ousting from the company he co-founded.

The Ground from Which It Grew: Apple's Rise

In the late 1970s and early 1980s, Apple quickly became a major player in the tech industry. Its early products, such as the Apple II, were some of the first personal computers to gain widespread success.

Jobs, as the face of Apple, played a key role in shaping the company's marketing and product development. His visionary leadership brought about the Macintosh in 1984 – the first commercially successful personal computer with a graphical user interface, making computers more accessible to a broad audience.

As Apple grew, so did internal tensions. Jobs was known for being a perfectionist, pushing his team to meet impossibly high standards. While this drive for excellence was key to Apple's innovations, it also created a toxic work environment.

Jobs frequently clashed with employees, dismissed others' ideas, and was unwilling to compromise, even when doing so would have benefited the company. This growing friction eventually led to conflict with Apple's board and leadership team.

Are there areas in your life where the pursuit of perfection may be straining your relationships or limiting collaboration?

Sowing the Seeds of Mistake

Jobs' downfall at Apple was the result of his inability to balance vision with collaboration. As Apple expanded, managing the company became more complex. Jobs, while laser-focused on innovation, struggled to lead effectively in this new environment.

In 1983, he personally recruited John Sculley, a PepsiCo executive, to help manage Apple's growth. However, the partnership quickly soured.

Jobs and Sculley often disagreed over the company's direction. Jobs felt that Apple was losing its creative edge, while Sculley and the board were increasingly frustrated with Jobs' management style.

In 1985, this tension reached its breaking point, and the board sided with Sculley, stripping Jobs of his operational role. Jobs, unwilling to work under these conditions, left the company he had helped build.

Jobs' removal wasn't simply the result of corporate politics; it was the consequence of his refusal to collaborate, listen to others, or manage his relationships. His visionary leadership was undeniable, but his inability to compromise and work with others led to his fall.

Are you actively listening to those around you and seeking their input, or are you letting your vision override collaboration?

Reaping What Was Sown

After leaving Apple, Jobs founded NeXT, a computer platform development company, and purchased Pixar, a small animation studio. While NeXT never achieved commercial success, the technology developed there eventually became foundational to Apple's modern operating systems.

Pixar, on the other hand, went on to revolutionise digital animation, with films like *Toy Story* becoming massive hits and cementing Jobs' legacy in yet another industry.

During his time away from Apple, Jobs learned valuable lessons about leadership. Both NeXT and Pixar gave him the opportunity to refine his approach, teaching him how to balance his visionary drive with improved management practices. Pixar, in particular, allowed Jobs to achieve a different kind of success, as it became one of the most successful animation studios in the world.

In 1997, Apple, struggling both financially and creatively, invited Jobs to return. Over the next decade, Jobs led Apple through its most successful period, introducing groundbreaking products like the iPod, iPhone, and iPad.

These innovations didn't just save Apple – they transformed entire industries. Jobs' return to Apple was a remarkable comeback, proving that his creative vision was integral to the company's success.

Despite his success during his second stint at Apple, Jobs' leadership flaws persisted. Though he had become better at managing relationships and collaborating with his team, his perfectionism and intensity still caused tension.

Former colleagues often described the pressure of working under him, though they also acknowledged that this pressure pushed the company to produce industry-defining products.

How do you balance pushing for excellence with creating an environment where collaboration and growth are possible for everyone?

Harvesting the Lessons

Steve Jobs' career exemplifies both the power of visionary thinking, and the pitfalls of arrogance and poor interpersonal skills. His early leadership at Apple was marked by innovation, but also by a rigid, demanding management style that alienated colleagues and led to his ousting from the company he co-founded.

However, his eventual return to Apple demonstrated his growth, as he combined his creative genius with a more collaborative approach, transforming Apple into a global powerhouse.

Jobs' story highlights the importance of balancing ambition with humility. Vision alone is not enough – true leadership requires listening to others, fostering teamwork, and adapting to feedback. His eventual success shows that learning from past mistakes, and evolving as a leader, can turn failures into the foundation for extraordinary achievements.

Jobs' journey reminds us that failure is often a stepping stone to growth. It challenges us to reflect on how we lead, work with others, and persevere through setbacks to realise our greatest potential.

Here are three scenarios to reflect on, with reflections to help apply these lessons to your own life:

Scenario 1: Prioritising Vision Over Collaboration

You're working on a creative project and feel strongly about your vision. However, others on your team have offered suggestions or feedback that don't align with your ideas. You find yourself brushing off their input, believing your way is best.

Reflection Questions:

- How often do you Prioritise your vision over collaboration?

- What might change if you considered others' perspectives or invited their feedback?

- How could balancing your ideas with collaboration strengthen the final outcome?

Scenario 2: Perfectionism in Everyday Tasks

You're organising your home, or completing a routine task, and you've been holding off finishing it because you want everything to be exactly right. Meanwhile, the task remains incomplete, and it's starting to weigh on your mind.

Reflection Questions:

- Are there areas in your daily life where striving for perfection is preventing progress?

- How might accepting small imperfections help make you feel more productive or at ease?

- What's one simple way to move forward without overthinking every detail?

Scenario 3: Learning From Mistakes and Adapting

You recently experienced a setback – a plan or project didn't turn out as expected. It's left you questioning your abilities or feeling hesitant to try again.

Reflection Questions:

- How do you typically respond to failure – by learning and adapting, or by retreating?

- What's one lesson you can take from this experience to improve your next effort?

- How might reframing failure as a growth opportunity change your approach to challenges?

Final Reflection

Jobs' story reminds us that leadership isn't just about having a vision – it's about balancing ambition with collaboration, embracing progress over perfection, and turning setbacks into growth. Consider:

- Are your actions fostering collaboration and progress, or are they holding you back?
- How might embracing imperfection and learning from mistakes open doors to greater success?

Tilling the Soil of Reflection

Steve Jobs' leadership story reminds us that vision alone isn't enough to ensure long-term success. While his creativity and drive were unparalleled, his refusal to collaborate, and his abrasive personality, initially led to his removal from Apple.

Are you prioritising collaboration and feedback? Are you creating a supportive environment for your team, or are you too focused on your personal vision?

Breaking New Ground

Imagine a master sculptor, chiselling away at a block of marble with intense focus and precision. Each strike shapes the stone closer to his vision, but his relentless pursuit of perfection leads him to strike too forcefully, causing cracks that threaten the integrity of the entire sculpture.

Steve Jobs, co-founder of Apple Inc, was akin to this sculptor – his visionary leadership and exacting standards propelled innovation, but sometimes fractured relationships and stifled collaboration within his teams. Jobs was renowned for his meticulous attention to detail, and a relentless drive for excellence.

However, his autocratic leadership style often manifested in harsh criticism and impatience, creating a work environment where employees felt undervalued and fearful of making mistakes.

This approach, while driving some to achieve greatness, also led to high employee turnover, and a culture where open communication was stifled.

Reflect on your leadership or collaborative experiences. Have you ever pushed so hard for perfection that it strained your relationships, or hindered team cohesion? Jobs' story prompts us to consider: Are we wielding our tools with care, or are we striking so hard that we risk shattering the very foundations we're trying to build?

Cultivating Growth

Steve Jobs' leadership style offers valuable lessons on the balance between pursuing excellence, and fostering a healthy, collaborative environment.

Key Takeaways:

- **Balance Precision with Empathy**: While high standards can drive innovation, it's crucial to balance them with empathy and support for your team. Recognise the human element in every endeavour.
- **Encourage Open Dialogue**: A culture where feedback flows freely, fosters growth and prevents the buildup of tension. Encourage your team to voice concerns and ideas without fear of harsh criticism.
- **Lead by Example, Not Intimidation**: Inspire your team through your actions and dedication, rather than through fear or coercion. Leadership rooted in respect cultivates loyalty and sustained success.

True growth emerges from the harmonious blend of vision and compassion. Steve Jobs' journey illustrates that, while a relentless pursuit of excellence can lead to groundbreaking achievements, it must be tempered with understanding and respect for those who help bring the vision to life.

Consider your own path: Are there areas where your drive for perfection has overshadowed the well-being of your team or relationships? How can you adjust your approach to ensure that your pursuit of excellence doesn't come at the expense of collaboration and mutual respect?

Growth isn't solely about achieving perfection; it's about sculpting an environment where innovation thrives alongside trust and camaraderie. Strike the balance carefully, and you'll create a masterpiece that stands the test of time.

PLANTING STAGE 9

Empress Dowager Cixi – The Empress Who Resisted Change

Quote: "I have often wished I had been born in another age, a time of less strife and fewer worries."
– Empress Dowager Cixi

Image: Empress Dowager Cixi, 1902. Photo by John Yu Shuinling. Public domain via Wikimedia Commons.

Before You Read:

Cixi ruled with force—but also fear of modernity. Her resistance to progress feels miles apart from Elon Musk's restlessness (Chapter 6), yet both show how power can distort our sense of timing. You might also revisit Marie Curie (Chapter 10), whose openness to risk changed everything—sometimes at a price.

Breaking Ground: The Power Behind the Throne

Empress Dowager Cixi was one of the most powerful and controversial figures in Chinese history.

Born in 1835, she rose from imperial concubine to effectively ruling China for nearly half a century during the late Qing Dynasty. Despite never officially being crowned Empress, Cixi wielded immense power, controlling imperial policies and the Chinese court from behind the throne.

Her reign coincided with a period of internal unrest and external pressure on China, as Western powers encroached and called for modernisation. While the Qing Dynasty struggled to maintain control, reformers pushed for changes to modernise the military, economy, and infrastructure.

However, Cixi was a deeply conservative leader who resisted these reforms, fearing that modernisation would undermine the Confucian order that had governed China for centuries.

Although Cixi did introduce reforms later in life, her initial resistance contributed to China's weakening in the face of foreign pressures. By the time she embraced change, it was too late to save the empire from its eventual collapse.

The Ground from Which It Grew: A Time of Decline and Crisis

During the 19th century, China faced a period of significant decline. The once-powerful Qing Dynasty was weakened by internal rebellions, like the Taiping Rebellion, and external threats, such as the Opium Wars with Britain, left China vulnerable to foreign exploitation.

By the time Cixi rose to power, China was being forced to open its ports to foreign trade, while its military remained outdated compared to the Western powers. Although reformers urged modernisation, Cixi resisted, clinging to traditional values and fearing that adopting Western practices would erode the empire's foundation. She believed that China's strength lay in its ancient traditions and Confucian order.

Cixi's reluctance to modernise stemmed from her desire to preserve power and control. Instead of investing in military and economic reforms, she diverted funds to personal projects, such as the construction of her lavish Summer Palace – a decision that would come back to haunt both her and the empire.

Are there areas in your life where clinging to the past or resisting change may be limiting your growth?

Sowing the Seeds of Mistake

Cixi's greatest mistake was her long-standing resistance to modernisation. While other nations, like Japan, were rapidly advancing their economies and militaries, Cixi clung to the past.

Her refusal to adopt Western technology and ideas left China weakened, unable to defend itself against foreign powers. This was most evident during the First Sino-Japanese War in 1895, where China lost control of Korea and Taiwan – crushing defeats that highlighted the empire's vulnerability.

One of the most notorious examples of Cixi's mismanagement was the Self-Strengthening Movement. Initially supported by reformers to modernise the military and infrastructure, Cixi ultimately undermined these efforts, fearing that Western influence would corrupt traditional values. Her conservative stance caused China to fall further behind its neighbours, leaving the empire increasingly vulnerable to foreign exploitation.

In 1900, Cixi made another grave mistake by supporting the Boxer Rebellion, a violent anti-foreign, anti-Christian uprising. Desperate to maintain control, she backed the Boxers in their attempt to drive out Western influences.

However, the rebellion ended disastrously, as an international coalition invaded China and forced the Qing Dynasty to pay massive reparations – further weakening the empire and isolating China from the global community.

By the time Cixi recognised the need for reform, the damage had already been done. While she introduced late-stage reforms to modernise the military and education system, these efforts were too little, too late. The Qing Dynasty collapsed just a few years after her death in 1908.

Are you resisting necessary change out of fear or a desire to maintain control? What might be the long-term consequences of delaying progress?

Reaping What Was Sown

The consequences of Cixi's resistance to change were profound. Her refusal to modernise China during the critical years of the late 19th century left the country vulnerable to foreign domination and internal strife. While other nations were advancing, China struggled to maintain its sovereignty and keep pace with a rapidly evolving world.

Although Cixi's late reforms aimed to modernise the empire, they could not reverse the damage caused by decades of stagnation. The Boxer

Rebellion further isolated China, drained its finances, and contributed to the empire's decline. The Qing Dynasty was left in disarray, losing support from both its people and the international community.

Cixi's legacy is one of missed opportunities. Her resistance to change, driven by fear of losing power, hastened the empire's fall. By the time she embraced modernisation, it was too late to save the Qing Dynasty. China would spend the next several decades in turmoil, leading to the establishment of the Republic of China and eventually the People's Republic of China.

Are there opportunities in your life that you're letting slip away because of hesitation or fear? What steps can you take to embrace change before it's too late?

Harvesting the Lessons

Empress Dowager Cixi's rule during China's late Qing Dynasty illustrates the complexities of power, resistance to change, and the dangers of short-term thinking. While she consolidated immense authority, and maintained control for decades, her reluctance to modernise China's economy, military, and political structures, left the empire vulnerable to foreign powers and internal unrest, ultimately contributing to its collapse.

Cixi's story serves as a reminder that clinging to traditional ways, while resisting progress, can hinder growth and stability. Leadership requires foresight, adaptability, and the courage to embrace necessary reforms, even when they challenge the status quo.

Today, Cixi's legacy teaches us the importance of balancing preservation with innovation. Her life reminds us that true strength lies not just in maintaining power, but in preparing for the future and creating systems that can thrive beyond our time.

Here are three scenarios to reflect on, with reflections to help apply these lessons to your own life:

Scenario 1: Resisting Change in Personal Growth

You've been avoiding a necessary change in your personal life – like improving a habit, adopting a healthier lifestyle, or learning a new skill. While the current approach feels comfortable, you know deep down that embracing this change could open up new opportunities or improve your well-being.

Reflection Questions:

- What fears or assumptions are holding you back from making this change?

- How might embracing the unknown lead to growth or improvement?

- What's one small step you can take to start this journey today?

Scenario 2: Adapting to New Circumstances in Professional Life

Your workplace or industry is evolving, requiring you to adopt new technology, processes, or skills. You feel hesitant, thinking the old ways have always worked fine for you, but you're starting to notice the gap between where you are and where you need to be.

Reflection Questions:

- How open are you to learning and adapting to new challenges in your professional life?

- What's at stake if you resist these changes, and how might embracing them strengthen your position?

- What's one way you can start adapting, whether through upskilling, seeking mentorship, or trying a new tool or method?

Scenario 3: Balancing Short-Term Gains with Long-Term Goals

You recently made a decision – perhaps financial, professional, or personal – that Prioritised short-term convenience over long-term benefits. Now, you're beginning to question if this approach aligns with your broader goals.

Reflection Questions:

- Are you considering the long-term consequences of your decisions, or are you focused on immediate results?

- How might prioritising the bigger picture impact your future positively?

- What's one adjustment you could make to align your decisions more closely with your long-term objectives?

Final Reflection

Cixi's story highlights the importance of adaptability, timely action, and thinking beyond short-term gains. As you reflect, consider:

- Are you resisting necessary changes, and what opportunities might you unlock by embracing them?
- How might adapting to change and focusing on long-term goals lead to greater success and fulfillment?

EMPRESS DOWAGER CIXI – THE EMPRESS WHO RESISTED CHANGE

Tilling the Soil of Reflection

Empress Dowager Cixi's legacy is a cautionary tale about the dangers of resisting change when the world around you is evolving. Her fear of losing control led to missed opportunities and, by the time she embraced reform, it was too late.

Are you resisting necessary changes in your life?

Breaking New Ground

Imagine a gardener who tends to a sprawling, ancient tree. The tree has deep roots, symbolising tradition and history, but its branches are withering, and its leaves are falling. The gardener, unwilling to trim the dead branches or plant new seeds, pours all her effort into preserving the tree as it is – hoping to keep it alive through sheer determination.

Empress Dowager Cixi's reign is much like this gardener's efforts: a leader focused on maintaining the grandeur of the Qing Dynasty while resisting the changes needed for it to thrive in a rapidly shifting world. Cixi's political mastery and ability to consolidate power allowed her to preserve the dynasty through turbulent times.

However, her reluctance to embrace reforms, and adapt to modernisation, left the empire vulnerable to external pressures and internal decay. Like the gardener clinging to the old tree, Cixi's decisions delayed the inevitable, weakening the foundations she worked so hard to protect.

Are there areas in your life where you're holding on to outdated practices or ideas, resisting the changes needed to grow? Cixi's story encourages us to ask: Are we nurturing growth, or are we simply trying to preserve what no longer serves us?

Cultivating Growth

Empress Dowager Cixi's story offers lessons on the importance of embracing change, and balancing tradition with innovation. Her legacy shows the risks of clinging too tightly to the past while neglecting the needs of the future.

Key Takeaways:

- **Prune for Growth**: Like a tree, systems and ideas need regular renewal. Letting go of what no longer serves can make room for new growth.
- **Balance Tradition with Progress**: Respecting history is important, but adapting to the present ensures survival and relevance in a changing world.
- **Act with Foresight**: Decisions rooted in short-term preservation can have long-term consequences. Prioritise sustainable actions that prepare for future challenges.

True growth comes from knowing when to let go of what is no longer working. Cixi's story reminds us that, while preserving the past is valuable, growth often requires bold decisions and a willingness to embrace change.

So, here's your challenge: Are you clinging to an "old tree" in your life, reluctant to trim away the dead branches? What steps can you take to nurture not just survival, but flourishing?

Growth is about balancing respect for tradition with a readiness to innovate, ensuring that what we build today stands strong for generations to come.

PLANTING STAGE 10

Marie Curie – The Cost of Dedication

Quote: "I was taught that the way of progress was neither swift nor easy."
– Marie Curie

Image: Marie Curie, circa 1898. Public domain (U.S.) via Wikimedia Commons.

Before You Read:

What are you willing to sacrifice for your work? Curie's commitment changed science—and took a toll. If you've reflected on Cixi (Chapter 9), you'll see how choosing comfort over risk can leave a legacy just as haunted. Or compare her to Jobs (Chapter 8), who also poured himself into invention, with mixed results.

Breaking Ground: The Groundbreaking Scientist

Marie Curie, born Maria Sklodowska in 1867 in Warsaw, Poland, stands as one of the most accomplished scientists in history.

Her pioneering research in radioactivity, alongside her husband Pierre Curie, earned her two Nobel Prizes – in Physics and Chemistry – making her the first woman to win a Nobel and the only person to win in two distinct scientific fields. Her discovery of radioactive elements, such as radium and polonium, revolutionised the scientific world and opened doors to groundbreaking advancements in medicine, including cancer treatment.

Curie's unwavering dedication to science shattered barriers for women in a male-dominated field, inspiring generations to follow in her footsteps. Her contributions laid the foundation for understanding atomic structures, radiation, and its medical applications.

However, her relentless pursuit of discovery also came at a great personal cost. The very substances she worked with ultimately contributed to her deteriorating health, serving as a reminder of the fine line between brilliance and personal sacrifice.

The Ground from Which It Grew: A Quest for Knowledge

At the turn of the 20th century, radioactivity was a largely unexplored field. Marie Curie's fascination with science began in her youth, despite limited opportunities for women in education at the time. Her determination led her to Paris, where she and her husband, Pierre, began investigating the properties of radioactive substances.

Their work led to the identification of two new elements – polonium and radium – ushering in a new era of scientific exploration. The Curies' discoveries were not just theoretical; they had practical applications that would transform industries and medicine.

However, Curie's intense dedication to her research often meant working long hours in makeshift laboratories, handling radioactive substances without protective measures. The full extent of radiation's harmful effects on the human body was unknown at the time, and Curie herself had no way of understanding the risks she faced.

Are you pursuing a goal so intensely that you might be overlooking potential risks to your well-being?

Sowing the Seeds of Mistake

Curie's greatest mistake was her failure to recognise the health risks associated with prolonged exposure to radiation. She and Pierre handled radioactive materials with little protection – often carrying vials of radium in their pockets, and working with radioactive substances in poorly ventilated labs.

The very notebooks, where Curie recorded her groundbreaking research, remain so radioactive today that they are stored in lead-lined boxes.

The lack of protective protocols, combined with the Curies' tireless commitment to their work, exposed them to dangerous levels of radiation for years. Curie's intense exposure led to a host of health problems, including chronic fatigue, cataracts, and, ultimately, aplastic anaemia – a condition that affects the bone marrow and is often linked to high levels of radiation exposure.

Curie's drive for progress blinded her to the potential dangers of her work. In her pursuit of scientific advancement, she overlooked the long-term effects of radiation on her health. This oversight was not just a product of the time, but also a reflection of the single-minded determination that had driven her to such great heights.

Are you so focused on achieving your goals that you might be ignoring warning signs that could affect your health or well-being?

Reaping What Was Sown

The consequences of Curie's exposure to radiation were severe. In 1934, at the age of 66, she succumbed to complications from aplastic anaemia, a condition widely believed to have been caused by her years of working with radioactive materials.

Her premature death was a direct result of her passion for scientific discovery, serving as both a cautionary tale and a mark of her incredible sacrifice.

Curie's legacy, however, is twofold. Her discoveries continue to benefit science and medicine, particularly in the field of radiotherapy for cancer treatment. Her work changed the world, but her personal story highlights the dangers of pushing the limits of scientific inquiry without proper safeguards.

Her death also marked a turning point in the scientific community's understanding of radiation. Following her passing, greater precautions were taken in the handling of radioactive materials, and stricter safety protocols were introduced to protect future generations of scientists from similar fates.

What safeguards are you putting in place to ensure your passion doesn't come at the cost of your well-being?

Harvesting the Lessons

Marie Curie's groundbreaking discoveries in radioactivity revolutionised science, but her work came with significant personal costs. Her long-term exposure to radiation, combined with the lack of understanding about its dangers at the time, led to health issues that eventually claimed her life.

Curie's story highlights the importance of balancing passion and dedication, with caution and self-care. While her commitment to advancing science was unmatched, it also serves as a reminder of the need to Prioritise one's well-being, even in the pursuit of great achievements.

Her legacy teaches us that passion and perseverance can change the world, but they must be paired with mindfulness and care for ourselves. Curie's life inspires us to chase our goals fearlessly, but also to protect the foundation – our health and well-being – that allows us to achieve them.

Here are three scenarios to reflect on, with reflections to help apply these lessons to your own life:

Scenario 1: Balancing Health and Ambition

You've been working long hours on a project or career goal, noticing signs of burnout – fatigue, stress, or neglect of personal relationships. While you feel your dedication is necessary, part of you wonders if it's sustainable.

Reflection Questions:

- Are you sacrificing your well-being to achieve your goals?

- What signs might indicate it's time to Prioritise self-care?

- How might setting boundaries or taking breaks improve your overall performance and well-being?

MARIE CURIE – THE COST OF DEDICATION

Scenario 2: Understanding Risks in Decision-Making

You're considering a significant decision, such as investing in a business venture, taking on a challenging role, or pursuing a bold personal goal. While it feels exciting, you realise you haven't fully assessed the potential risks or downsides.

Reflection Questions:

- Are you fully informed about the risks involved in your choices?

- How can educating yourself, or seeking advice, help you anticipate and mitigate potential challenges?

- What's one proactive step you can take to ensure your decision is well-informed and balanced?

Scenario 3: Recognising When to Reassess

You're deeply enthusiastic about a cause or project and have been pushing yourself to meet an ambitious goal. Despite your enthusiasm, signs of diminishing returns – fatigue, frustration, or stalled progress – are becoming evident, but you're reluctant to slow down.

Reflection Questions:

- Are you noticing signs that it might be time to pause or reassess your approach?

- How could stepping back occasionally help sustain your energy and progress over the long term?

- What adjustments could you make to ensure your passion doesn't come at the cost of your well-being?

Final Reflection

Curie's story reminds us that passion and ambition should be balanced with health, caution, and sustainability. As you reflect, consider:

- Are you prioritising your well-being alongside your goals?
- How might stepping back, understanding risks, and reassessing your approach, lead to greater long-term success and fulfillment?

Tilling the Soil of Reflection

Marie Curie's life invites us to reflect on our own pursuit of success. Are we, like Curie, so focused on our goals that we fail to see the risks? Are we taking care of our well-being, or are we pushing ourselves to the point of personal harm? Her story reminds us that while ambition is vital, it must be balanced with self-care and awareness of the potential dangers we may face.

Breaking New Ground

Imagine a candle burning brightly in a dark room, its light illuminating everything around it. The flame is steady, determined, and unwavering. But, as it burns, the wax melts, the wick shortens, and the candle itself diminishes. Marie Curie's life reflects this metaphor; a brilliant scientist whose relentless dedication to her work illuminated the path for others but came at great personal cost.

Curie's groundbreaking discoveries in radioactivity revolutionised science and earned her two Nobel Prizes, yet her tireless pursuit of knowledge exposed her to radiation that ultimately compromised her health. Like the candle burning brightly, her work brought light to the world, but slowly consumed her in the process. Her story challenges us to reflect on how we balance passion and self-sacrifice, ensuring that our dedication doesn't come at the cost of our well-being.

Have you ever been so focused on a goal that you neglected your health or personal needs? Curie's story asks us to consider: Are we burning too brightly, risking ourselves in the process, or are we finding ways to sustain our flame for the long term?

Cultivating Growth

Marie Curie's story is a powerful reminder of the importance of balancing passion with self-care. While her work has left an enduring legacy, her sacrifices highlight the need to protect our well-being even as we strive for greatness.

Key Takeaways:

- **Sustain Your Flame**: Dedication is admirable, but burnout can limit your ability to contribute over the long term. Protect your well-being to sustain your impact.
- **Know When to Rest**: Even the brightest minds need time to recharge. Prioritise rest and renewal to maintain your energy and focus.
- **Value Collaboration**: Great achievements are rarely accomplished alone. Seek support and share the burden to lighten your load and expand your potential.

True growth lies in learning how to balance passion with sustainability. Curie's story inspires us to pursue our goals with determination, but it also serves as a cautionary tale about the risks of sacrificing too much in the name of achievement.

So, here's your challenge: Are you burning your candle too brightly, sacrificing your health or happiness for your goals? How can you adjust your pace or seek support to ensure your flame continues to shine?

Growth isn't about burning out – it's about finding a way to light the world while preserving yourself. Protect your flame, and you'll illuminate not only your path but the paths of others for years to come.

PART 3
INSPIRATIONAL TURNAROUNDS – SEEDS OF REDEMPTION

In the journey of life, mistakes are inevitable. For some, these mistakes lead to complete ruin, as we've seen in earlier chapters. But for others, failure becomes the catalyst for growth, transformation, and redemption.

These individuals did not let their mistakes define them. Instead, they used their failures as stepping stones toward something greater, reshaping their lives, and in some cases, the world around them.

In this final part of the book, we explore the stories of five remarkable figures who faced profound setbacks, yet found a way to rise above them. Each of these individuals made serious errors in judgment – errors that could have ended their careers, damaged their reputations, or derailed their personal lives. But instead of succumbing to these failures, they used them as opportunities to learn, grow, and ultimately thrive.

These figures serve as living proof that mistakes, no matter how significant, don't have to be the end of the story. Whether through personal reflection, a change in perspective, or sheer determination, they found a way to turn failure into fuel for success. Their stories remind us that while failure may feel like a dead end, it can actually be the beginning of a new chapter – one of growth, transformation, and redemption.

Each story illustrates a unique path to redemption:

- **Akio Morita**, the innovator, recovered from early business failures to found Sony, transforming global technology.
- **Nelson Mandela**, the leader, moved from violent resistance to become a global symbol of forgiveness and peace.
- **Winston Churchill**, the resilient statesman, turned his World War I Gallipoli disaster into lessons that shaped his leadership in Britain's darkest hour.
- **Oskar Schindler**, the profiteer, went from exploiting war to saving lives and becoming a Holocaust hero.
- **Alfred Nobel**, the inventor, transformed his legacy from destruction to one of peace and progress through the Nobel Prizes.

As you read these stories, consider how you can apply their lessons to your own life. How can you turn your own mistakes into opportunities for growth? What steps can you take to ensure that your failures lead to personal transformation rather than defeat?

These individuals exemplify the resilience of the human spirit. They show us that redemption is possible, and that even the darkest moments can lead to brighter futures. Their mistakes, like fertiliser, became the nutrients that allowed them to grow stronger and achieve even greater things.

In this section, you'll see how failure doesn't have to be final – it can be the beginning of a powerful turnaround.

What mistakes in your own life might hold the seeds for your next chapter of growth?

PLANTING STAGE 11

Akio Morita – Betting Everything on a Bold Vision

Quote: "Don't be afraid to make a mistake.
But make sure you don't make the same mistake twice."
– Akio Morita

Image: Akio Morita, circa 1982. Public domain (Japan) via Wikimedia Commons.

Before You Read:

Morita didn't get it right the first time—but he adapted. If you've looked at Musk (Chapter 6) or Zuckerberg (Chapter 7), this chapter offers a gentler kind of innovation: thoughtful, disciplined, and humble. Or contrast him with Napoleon (Chapter 2), who couldn't pivot when it mattered most.

Breaking Ground: The Visionary Behind Sony

Akio Morita, born in 1921 in Nagoya, Japan, was the son of a wealthy family involved in saké brewing. Despite his privileged background, Morita followed his passion for technology and electronics.

In 1946, in the aftermath of World War II, Morita co-founded Sony with Masaru Ibuka. What started as a small electronics company eventually grew into one of the world's largest and most innovative corporations.

Initially, Sony focused on producing simple electronics, but Morita had a bigger vision. He believed that Japanese products could compete on the global stage, and he set out to prove it. Early successes with transistors and radios helped establish Sony as a leader in innovation.

However, it was Morita's bold – and risky – decision to introduce a new product that would not only transform Sony's fortunes, but also change how people experience music around the world.

The Ground from Which It Grew: Post-War Japan and the Electronics Boom

In the 1960s and 1970s, the world was entering a period of rapid technological advancement. Electronics' companies were fiercely competing to create the next breakthrough, and Sony was part of this wave.

Morita was known for his daring business approach, pushing Sony to not just meet current consumer demands, but to create revolutionary products.

However, this ambitious approach came with significant risks. Sony often invested heavily in products that were ahead of their time, or seemed too unconventional. Morita's strategy was not just to fulfill needs but to anticipate them, a mindset that led to both failures and successes. This daring philosophy culminated in one of Sony's biggest gambles – the Sony Walkman.

Are you anticipating future opportunities, or are you focused only on immediate needs? What might you achieve by taking a bold step toward the future?

Sowing the Seeds of Mistake

The development of the Walkman began as a risky endeavour. When Ibuka first proposed the idea of a portable cassette player, many Sony executives were sceptical. The device didn't record audio, which was a feature that consumers expected at the time, and the market for a playback-only device seemed uncertain. The internal debate was intense, with many questioning whether there would be any demand for such a product.

Despite the doubts, Morita pushed forward, believing the Walkman could change how people listened to music. He envisioned a future where people would want a portable device to enjoy their favourite songs anywhere, anytime.

However, this decision was a major gamble for Sony. The company invested heavily in its production and, if the Walkman failed, Sony's financial stability and reputation could suffer.

When the Walkman launched in 1979, initial sales were disappointing, and critics were quick to label it a failure. The press questioned the practicality of a device that couldn't record, and early marketing efforts failed to convince consumers of its value. For a brief moment, it seemed like Morita's bold bet on the Walkman was a mistake.

Are there risks you're hesitating to take because of fear of failure? What would happen if you trusted your vision, even in the face of doubt?

Reaping What Was Sown

However, as time passed, Morita's vision proved correct. Consumers began to appreciate the convenience of portable music, and word of mouth spread quickly. What had seemed like a niche product soon became a global sensation. Sales surged, and the Walkman became a cultural icon, revolutionising how people experienced music.

The Walkman's success cemented Sony's reputation as a pioneer in innovation. It was more than just a product – it sparked a cultural shift that paved the way for future personal entertainment devices, like the Discman, the iPod, and other portable technologies. Morita's gamble demonstrated that bold, forward-thinking decisions could lead to industry-defining success.

Under Morita's leadership, Sony continued to innovate, launching products like the PlayStation, which would go on to transform the gaming industry. His legacy at Sony was one of visionary leadership, calculated risks, and resilience in the face of doubt.

Are you allowing short-term setbacks to define your path, or are you willing to push through to realise your long-term vision? How can you build resilience in the face of doubt?

Harvesting the Lessons

Akio Morita, the co-founder of Sony, demonstrated the importance of resilience and adaptability in the face of failure. Sony's first product, an early rice cooker, was a commercial flop, burning rice instead of cooking it properly.

However, Morita and his team didn't let this setback define them. They learned from the experience, pivoted their focus to electronics, and ultimately revolutionised the industry with innovations like the Walkman and the transistor radio.

Morita's story is a testament to viewing failure not as the end, but as a stepping stone toward future success. His willingness to embrace mistakes and adapt his vision underscores the value of persistence and creative thinking.

These lessons remain relevant for anyone today; setbacks are not roadblocks but opportunities to refine your approach and push forward. Morita's journey encourages us to stay determined, take calculated risks, and turn failures into platforms for success.

Here are three scenarios to reflect on, with reflections to help apply these lessons to your own life:

Scenario 1: Balancing Risk with Preparation

You're considering making a significant change – like switching careers, starting a business, or taking on a leadership role. The opportunity feels exciting, but you're unsure if you're adequately prepared to succeed.

Reflection Questions:

- How can you balance taking risks with being thoughtful and prepared?

- What's one resource, skill, or support system you could seek out to strengthen your confidence?

- How might taking this step, even with uncertainty, push you closer to your long-term goals?

Scenario 2: Anticipating Future Opportunities

You're managing a team, or planning your career path, and most of your energy goes into solving present challenges. You realise you haven't been thinking ahead to where your industry, relationships, or goals might evolve in the next few years.

Reflection Questions:

- Are you spending enough time anticipating future opportunities, or are you just reacting to current needs?

- How might forward-thinking improve your ability to adapt and succeed?

- What's one way you can start preparing for the future today, such as learning a new skill, or analysing emerging trends?

Scenario 3: Taking Responsibility for Bold Decisions

You're faced with a significant decision that could shape your career, family, or personal growth. While the potential rewards are great, so are the risks, and you're unsure if you're ready to take full accountability for the outcome.

Reflection Questions:

- How does taking responsibility for your decisions strengthen your leadership or personal growth?

- What's one way you can shift from hesitation to ownership of the choice you're considering?

- How might stepping into accountability empower you to move forward confidently?

Final Reflection

Morita's story reminds us that success often comes from taking bold risks, anticipating future needs, and owning the outcomes of our decisions. As you reflect, consider:

- Are you ready to trust your vision and embrace the uncertainty of pursuing it?

- How might thinking ahead and taking accountability help you grow as a leader and innovator?

Tilling the Soil of Reflection

Akio Morita's story encourages us to reflect on our approach to risk. Are we willing to take bold steps, even if success isn't guaranteed? Do we have the perseverance to push through setbacks? Morita's journey reminds us that innovation and success often come from daring to challenge the norm, and pushing beyond conventional limits.

Breaking New Ground

Imagine a craftsman meticulously creating a fine piece of technology, one detail at a time. He envisions a product that will not only stand the test of time but also change the way people live. But in his pursuit of perfection, he can sometimes overlook the needs of his team, or the evolving market around him. Akio Morita, the co-founder of Sony, is a figure who, much like this craftsman, built an empire based on innovation and attention to detail – but his path was not without challenges.

Morita's vision helped create Sony's global success, introducing products that revolutionised the electronics industry, from the Walkman to the PlayStation. However, as Sony grew, Morita's focus on innovation sometimes clashed with the realities of an evolving market.

His commitment to quality and perfectionism, while admirable, occasionally slowed the company's response to shifts in technology and consumer demands. Like a craftsman focused solely on the minute details, Morita's story reminds us that even the best-crafted products need to evolve with time and the changing needs of those they serve.

Have you ever been so focused on perfecting a project that you missed the bigger picture, or failed to adapt to a new environment? Morita's story invites us to ask: Are we so committed to our vision that we overlook the need to adjust and adapt as circumstances change?

Cultivating Growth

Akio Morita's legacy is one of innovation and excellence, but his story also teaches us the importance of balancing perfection with adaptability. While the desire for quality and precision is essential, it must be coupled with an awareness of the market, the people, and the world around us.

Key Takeaways:

- **Adapt to Change**: Innovation is key, but staying static in a dynamic world can lead to stagnation. Be ready to pivot and adapt your ideas to meet evolving demands.
- **Balance Perfection with Practicality**: While striving for excellence is important, perfectionism can sometimes hinder progress. Know when 'good' is enough to keep moving forward.
- **Collaborate and Listen**: As your vision grows, so does the need for teamwork. Stay attuned to the insights and feedback of others to ensure your product or project stays relevant and effective.

True growth is about striking the balance between the pursuit of excellence and the ability to evolve. Akio Morita's story reminds us that, while innovation and attention to detail can create lasting success, we must also be open to change, and to be responsive to the world around us.

So, here's your challenge: Are there areas in your life where perfectionism, or a rigid focus on your vision, may be hindering your ability to adapt?

How can you open yourself up to new ideas, changes, or feedback to ensure that your work continues to grow and evolve?

Growth is about creating something lasting, but also knowing when to evolve, adjust, and let go of perfection in order to embrace the future. Keep your craft sharp, but also stay open to the ever-changing landscape around you.

PLANTING STAGE 12

Nelson Mandela – The Power of Forgiveness

Quote: "Resentment is like drinking poison and then hoping it will kill your enemies."
– Nelson Mandela

Image: Nelson Mandela (1994) by John Mathew Smith. Licensed under CC BY-SA 2.0 via Wikimedia Commons.

NELSON MANDELA – THE POWER OF FORGIVENESS

Before You Read:

Mandela's life is the clearest proof that mistakes don't define you—what you do next does. If you started with Ned Kelly (Chapter 1), this is a powerful counterpoint: two men resisting oppression, but only one willing to evolve. Or contrast him with Nixon (Chapter 3), who couldn't let go of control long enough to earn redemption.

Breaking Ground: The Revolutionary Leader

Nelson Mandela was born in 1918 in rural South Africa, a country deeply divided by racial segregation and apartheid.

From a young age, Mandela was drawn to the fight for racial equality, studying law and joining the African National Congress (ANC), where he became a key figure in the movement to end apartheid. Initially, Mandela advocated for peaceful resistance but, as the oppressive regime intensified its efforts to suppress the black population, he eventually supported armed struggle as a means to achieve liberation.

Mandela's leadership in the militant wing of the ANC, *Umkhonto we Sizwe*, led to his arrest in 1962. Convicted of sabotage and conspiracy to overthrow the government, Mandela was sentenced to life in prison. For many, this could have been the end of his story – a revolutionary silenced by imprisonment.

However, Mandela's time behind bars became a turning point in his life, where his approach to leadership, resistance, and reconciliation, was fundamentally transformed.

The Ground from Which It Grew: A Nation Divided

During Mandela's imprisonment, South Africa remained a country ruled by racial apartheid. The black majority was denied basic human rights, segregated into impoverished communities, and subjected to brutal oppression by the white minority government. The ANC continued its fight for freedom, but the country teetered on the verge of civil war.

From Robben Island, where Mandela spent 18 of his 27 years in prison, he had time to reflect on the cycle of violence consuming his nation. Though he had once supported armed resistance, Mandela began to realise that violence could not build the peaceful, unified country he dreamed of. He saw that the only way forward was through reconciliation, not revenge.

In moments of division, how do you approach conflict? Do you strive for unity, or do you allow frustration to guide your actions?

Sowing the Seeds of Mistake

Mandela's early support of violent resistance, though born from understandable frustration with the injustice of apartheid, became one of his biggest mistakes. The turn to violence divided the resistance movement, alienated potential allies, and played into the government's narrative that the ANC was a threat to national security.

During his years in prison, Mandela reconsidered his approach. He realised that while the apartheid regime's oppression had to be fought, violence would only perpetuate the hatred and divisions that tore South Africa apart. He saw that in order to lead his country toward real and lasting change, he needed to embrace a different kind of leadership – one rooted in forgiveness and unity.

This realisation didn't come easily. It took years of reflection, dialogue, and personal transformation. By the time Mandela was released from prison in 1990, he had become a different kind of leader – one whose vision for South Africa went beyond liberation to reconciliation. He was no longer the fiery revolutionary calling for armed resistance; he had become the statesman who would lead South Africa toward peace.

How do you react when you realise your current path isn't leading to the outcome you desire? Are you open to re-evaluating and changing direction?

Reaping What Was Sown

Mandela's embrace of forgiveness, rather than vengeance, became the foundation for South Africa's transition to democracy. Upon his release, he could have called for retaliation against the white minority government but, instead, he chose a path of peace.

Mandela's leadership during this delicate period was marked by his ability to unite a deeply divided nation, advocating for reconciliation between blacks and whites.

In 1994, Mandela was elected as South Africa's first black president in the country's first fully democratic elections. Rather than seeking revenge for the decades of suffering inflicted under apartheid, Mandela worked to heal the wounds of the past.

His establishment of the Truth and Reconciliation Commission, which allowed victims and perpetrators of apartheid-era violence to share their stories, was a testament to his commitment to healing the nation.

Mandela's legacy is one of forgiveness, compassion, and unity. His decision to turn away from violence, and instead embrace reconciliation, changed the course of South African history. The peaceful transition to democracy, something many thought impossible, was made possible because Mandela chose forgiveness over retribution.

How can forgiveness and reconciliation play a role in resolving your own conflicts? What impact might these choices have on the world around you?

Harvesting the Lessons

Nelson Mandela's early years as an activist and leader of the African National Congress saw him turn to armed resistance against apartheid, leading to his imprisonment for 27 years.

While in prison, Mandela reflected deeply on his approach, emerging with a renewed commitment to reconciliation and non-violence. His ability to transform personal hardship into a powerful platform for unity ultimately led to the end of apartheid, and to his presidency.

Mandela's story teaches us that strength lies not just in standing against injustice, but in finding ways to heal and unite after the fight. His willingness to adapt, forgive, and lead with compassion, turned potential division into a foundation for lasting change.

The lessons of Mandela's life remind us that even in the face of oppression, transformation and reconciliation are possible. His journey challenges us to approach conflict with empathy, courage, and a vision for a better future.

Here are three scenarios to reflect on, with reflections to help apply these lessons to your own life:

Scenario 1: Letting Go of Resentment

You've been holding onto bitterness from a past conflict or betrayal. While the situation no longer affects your daily life, you find yourself revisiting the resentment, and it weighs on your emotional well-being.

Reflection Questions:

- What might you gain by letting go of this resentment?

- How could forgiveness open the door to personal growth and freedom?

- What small step can you take to begin releasing this weight?

Scenario 2: Choosing Reconciliation Over Retaliation

You've had a disagreement with a colleague, friend, or family member, and you're tempted to focus on proving you're right. The conflict is escalating, but you recognise an opportunity to Prioritise resolution over retaliation.

Reflection Questions:

- How do you typically handle conflicts – by seeking understanding or by trying to win?

- What impact has prioritising peace and reconciliation had on your relationships in the past?

- What's one action you can take to shift this situation toward mutual understanding?

Scenario 3: Learning from Past Mistakes as a Leader

You're in a position of influence – whether in your work, community, or family – and a recent challenge reminded you of a similar situation where things didn't go well. Reflecting on that earlier experience, you wonder how you can approach things differently this time.

Reflection Questions:

- What lessons from past mistakes or challenges can guide you in this situation?

- How might applying these lessons help you grow as a leader or decision-maker?

- What's one way you can demonstrate the growth you've gained from reflecting on past experiences?

Final Reflection

Mandela's story shows us that true strength lies in forgiveness, reconciliation, and growth. As you reflect, ask yourself:

- How can letting go of resentment or prioritising peace transform your relationships?
- What lessons from your past can help you lead with more compassion and courage in the future?

Tilling the Soil of Reflection

Nelson Mandela's life challenges us to reflect on how we handle our own conflicts and failures. Are we holding on to grudges that prevent us from growing? Are we choosing division over unity? Mandela's story reminds us that true leadership lies in our ability to bring people together, even after great hardship, and to find strength in forgiveness.

Breaking New Ground

Imagine a leader standing before a vast, turbulent sea. The waves crash against the shore, and the storm is fierce. The leader's mission is clear – to guide his people to safety and create a lasting change – but the road ahead is fraught with obstacles.

Nelson Mandela's life reflects this imagery, as he navigated the fierce storm of apartheid, guided by his vision of freedom, justice, and equality for all South Africans.

Mandela's journey was one of immense personal sacrifice. From his early activism to his imprisonment for 27 years, he faced challenges that would have broken many others.

Yet, throughout it all, he maintained a focus on his vision for a racially unified and democratic South Africa. His resilience and commitment to peace eventually led to the dismantling of apartheid, and his election as the country's first Black president.

However, Mandela's path was not without difficulty – his long imprisonment and personal sacrifices came at the cost of time, relationships, and health.

Mandela's story teaches us that true leadership often requires navigating through profound hardship and sacrifice. But it also asks: Are we prepared to endure the storms of our own struggles to see the broader vision through?

Cultivating Growth

Nelson Mandela's life offers profound lessons in perseverance, sacrifice, and the power of forgiveness. While his fight for justice was marked by tremendous personal cost, it also highlights the importance of staying focused on a greater purpose, even when faced with adversity.

Key Takeaways:

- **Endurance Through Adversity**: True leadership is about staying committed to your vision, even in the face of overwhelming challenges. Persistence is key to lasting change.
- **Sacrifice for a Greater Good**: Achieving monumental change often requires personal sacrifice. It's important to keep the greater good in mind when facing difficult decisions.
- **The Power of Forgiveness**: Mandela's capacity to forgive his oppressors and work toward reconciliation taught us that true strength lies in letting go of anger for the sake of unity and progress.

True growth is about enduring hardship with a sense of purpose, knowing that the struggles you face can lead to a greater outcome. Mandela's life exemplifies the strength it takes to endure personal sacrifices and still rise above, creating lasting change for the betterment of others.

So, here's your challenge: Are you willing to endure the storms of your own challenges for a greater vision? How can you align your struggles with a larger purpose, ensuring that your journey is not only about personal gain but about creating something that will benefit others in the long run?

Growth isn't just about achieving success – it's about remaining steadfast in your beliefs, and acting with integrity, even when faced with great adversity. Like Mandela, true growth lies in leading with conviction and working toward unity, no matter the cost.

PLANTING STAGE 13

Winston Churchill – The Man Who Bounced Back from Failure

Quote: "Success is not final; failure is not fatal: it is the courage to continue that counts."
– Winston Churchill

Image: Winston Churchill, original photo from Flickr. Licensed under CC BY 2.0 via Wikimedia Commons.

WINSTON CHURCHILL – THE MAN WHO BOUNCED BACK FROM FAILURE

Before You Read:

Churchill's story is for anyone who's failed publicly—and had to win back trust. If Nixon (Chapter 3) left you wondering how leaders recover from a fall, this chapter offers an answer. Or see how he compares to Steve Jobs (Chapter 8), another comeback story that required both grit and humility.

Breaking Ground: The Resilient Leader

Winston Churchill is remembered as one of the most influential leaders of the 20th century, a man whose indomitable spirit led Britain through its darkest hours during World War II.

Born into an aristocratic family in 1874, Churchill had a long and eventful political career that saw both spectacular successes, and crushing failures. His resilience and ability to rise after defeat are central to his legacy.

However, before becoming the iconic wartime prime minister, Churchill faced one of the most humiliating failures of his career – the disastrous Gallipoli Campaign during World War I. This military debacle not only cost thousands of lives but also nearly destroyed Churchill's political career.

Yet, in true Churchillian fashion, he did not allow this failure to define him. Instead, he used it as fuel for growth, eventually returning to lead Britain through the much more challenging ordeal of World War II.

The Ground from Which It Grew: A Nation in Crisis

In the early 20th century, Churchill had already established himself as a charismatic and ambitious political leader.

In 1915, during World War I, Churchill served as the First Lord of the Admiralty, responsible for naval strategy. At the time, the war was bogged down in a bloody stalemate on the Western Front, and Churchill believed that a bold naval offensive could turn the tide of the war. He advocated for a campaign against the Ottoman Empire at Gallipoli, a strategic point that could potentially open a new front and relieve pressure on the Western Allies.

Churchill's vision was grand, but the execution of the plan was deeply flawed. The Gallipoli Campaign became one of the most infamous failures in British military history. Poor planning, logistical failures, and underestimating the enemy, led to a disastrous outcome, with heavy Allied casualties and no strategic gains.

The failure at Gallipoli left Churchill politically isolated, and he was forced to resign from his post, tarnishing his reputation.

When faced with obstacles, do you focus on your vision without considering the practical challenges? Are you prepared to adapt when plans go awry?

Sowing the Seeds of Mistake

Churchill's mistake at Gallipoli stemmed from a combination of overconfidence and misjudgement. He believed that a swift naval victory would break the deadlock of trench warfare, but he did not fully account for the complexity of the operation, or the strength of the Ottoman defences. The campaign became a quagmire, with Allied forces facing fierce resistance and harsh conditions.

For Churchill, the failure at Gallipoli was a bitter pill to swallow. His ambition and desire for a decisive victory had led him to push for a risky, and ultimately doomed, strategy. The fallout from the failure was immense – thousands of soldiers died, and Churchill's career seemed to be in ruins. He was scapegoated for the disaster, and his political enemies used the failure to force him out of power.

But rather than letting this defeat break him, Churchill took the time to reflect on his mistakes. He understood that while his vision had been bold, his execution had been flawed. This period of political exile became a time of personal growth for Churchill, one that would later shape his leadership style during World War II.

Are you letting ambition cloud your judgment? How can you ensure that your plans are grounded in reality, without sacrificing boldness?

Reaping What Was Sown

The consequences of Gallipoli were devastating for both Churchill and the Allied forces. Churchill faced intense public criticism, was removed from his position, and suffered a deep personal and professional humiliation. Many thought his political career was over.

However, Churchill's story didn't end in defeat. After Gallipoli, he left the government and briefly served on the Western Front as an officer in the British Army. This period away from politics allowed him to reflect, regroup, and ultimately emerge stronger. His experiences in World War I, including the lessons learned from Gallipoli, prepared him for the monumental challenges he would face in World War II.

When the world found itself again on the brink of disaster in 1939, Churchill was called upon to lead. His famous speeches, unwavering resolve, and ability to learn from his past mistakes, made him the ideal leader to guide Britain through its darkest hours.

The lessons from Gallipoli stayed with him – he approached leadership with a renewed understanding of the consequences of overconfidence and poor planning. He became the steadfast symbol of British resilience, famously declaring, "We shall never surrender".

When you face failure, do you use it as an opportunity for growth, or do you let it define you? What lessons can you take from past mistakes to strengthen your resolve?

Harvesting the Lessons

Winston Churchill's early political career was marred by setbacks, including his role in the disastrous Gallipoli campaign during World War I, which led to his demotion and tarnished his reputation.

However, Churchill used these failures as opportunities to learn and grow, ultimately returning to lead Britain through its darkest hours during World War II with resilience and determination.

Churchill's story reminds us that failure is not the end – it's a chance to rebuild. His ability to persevere through personal and professional setbacks demonstrates that success often requires grit, self-reflection, and a refusal to give up.

The lessons from Churchill's life are clear: setbacks can strengthen us if we allow them to teach us. His journey encourages us to face challenges with courage, adapt when needed, and keep moving forward, even in the face of adversity.

Here are three scenarios to reflect on, with reflections to help apply these lessons to your own life:

WINSTON CHURCHILL – THE MAN WHO BOUNCED BACK FROM FAILURE

Scenario 1: Turning Failure into Growth

You've recently faced a setback in your personal or professional life. It's been weighing on your mind, and you're unsure how to move forward without letting it define you.

Reflection Questions:

- Do you view failure as an opportunity to grow, or does it hold you back?

- What lessons might you be overlooking in this setback?

- How can applying these lessons help you move forward with a stronger mindset?

Scenario 2: Seeking Input and Avoiding Overconfidence

You're preparing to make an important decision – at work, in a relationship, or in a personal project. While you feel confident in your choice, part of you wonders if you've fully considered all the alternatives, or sought enough feedback.

Reflection Questions:

- How often do you rely solely on your perspective when making decisions?

- When was the last time seeking advice or input helped you avoid a misstep?

- What's one way you could bring more collaboration into your decision-making process?

Scenario 3: Resilience in the Face of Adversity

You're currently navigating a difficult challenge – something that feels daunting or overwhelming. While the obstacles feel significant, you're determined to push through and emerge stronger.

Reflection Questions:

- How do you typically respond to adversity – by shying away or facing it head-on?

- What past experiences have shown you that you're capable of overcoming challenges?

- How can reframing this adversity as a stepping stone help you take the next step forward?

Final Reflection

Churchill's journey reminds us that failure is a powerful teacher, and resilience is built through reflection and persistence. As you reflect, consider:

- How can you use your setbacks as opportunities for learning and growth?
- What steps can you take today to approach challenges with courage and openness?

Tilling the Soil of Reflection

Winston Churchill's life demonstrates that failure, no matter how public or painful, doesn't have to be the end of the story. His journey from the humiliation of Gallipoli to leading Britain through World War II reminds us that resilience isn't about avoiding failure but about learning from it, and moving forward with wisdom and strength

How do you respond to your failures? Do you let them define you, or do you see them as opportunities to grow and improve?

Breaking New Ground

Imagine a general standing on the battlefield, the weight of the nation's fate resting on his shoulders. The enemy is strong, and the odds seem insurmountable, but the general's resolve remains unshaken. His leadership, though questioned by many, stands firm as he inspires his people to persevere. Winston Churchill's life mirrors this scenario, as he led Britain through the dark days of World War II, navigating a nation on the brink of collapse.

Churchill's career was filled with moments of triumph, but it was also marked by periods of failure and uncertainty. His leadership during the war, especially during Britain's darkest hours, was characterised by his unyielding belief in victory, even when all seemed lost.

Yet, his path was not without mistakes or misjudgements. His stubbornness, pride, and sometimes divisive rhetoric alienated allies and caused political strife. Churchill's leadership teaches us that sometimes the hardest battles are not just fought on the frontlines but in the struggle to maintain faith in the face of adversity.

Have you ever been in a position where the weight of responsibility felt unbearable, yet you had to press forward, despite doubts and criticism?

Churchill's story challenges us to consider: Are we willing to stand firm in our beliefs, even when the odds are against us?

Cultivating Growth

Winston Churchill's legacy is one of resilience, leadership, and unwavering resolve. His story shows us the value of perseverance, even when others doubt our vision or ability. However, it also serves as a reminder of the importance of humility and self-awareness in leadership.

Key Takeaways:

- **Stand Firm in Adversity**: Leadership often requires making tough decisions in the face of overwhelming odds. Confidence in your vision is essential, but so is the ability to inspire others to join you in that vision.
- **Embrace the Lessons of Failure**: Churchill's story teaches us that mistakes and failures are part of the journey. They offer valuable lessons that can make us stronger and more effective in the long run.
- **The Power of Words**: Churchill's speeches were instrumental in rallying the British people. His words had the power to lift spirits and galvanise a nation, showing us that how we communicate during crises can shape outcomes.

True growth isn't about always having the perfect strategy or being free from mistakes – it's about standing firm in the face of challenges, learning from failures, and using our strengths to guide others toward a shared vision. Churchill's story reminds us that leadership is about more than just personal success; it's about inspiring others to keep moving forward when they feel they can't go on.

MISTAKES ARE LIKE FERTILISER

So, here's your challenge: Are you ready to stand firm in your beliefs, even when others doubt you? How can you use your setbacks as stepping stones to grow stronger, more effective, and more inspiring?

Growth is about persistence, resilience, and the willingness to face difficult truths while continuing to lead others through adversity. Like Churchill, true growth requires both strength and humility, the courage to lead in dark times, and the wisdom to learn from the past.

PLANTING STAGE 14

Oskar Schindler – The Profiteer Who Became a Hero

Quote: "Whoever saves one life, saves the world entire."
– Oskar Schindler

Image: Oskar Schindler. Public domain (Argentina/U.S.) via Wikimedia Commons.

Before You Read:

If you've ever wondered if people really change, Schindler's story will challenge your assumptions. He began as a war profiteer. By the end, he'd saved over a thousand lives. For another radical shift, revisit Alfred Nobel (Chapter 15)—or contrast him with Cixi (Chapter 9), who clung to comfort rather than face change.

Breaking Ground: The Businessman Turned Savior

Oskar Schindler was a man of contradictions – a German businessman and Nazi Party member who, in the face of unimaginable horror, transformed into a saviour of over 1,200 Jewish lives during the Holocaust.

Born in 1908 in what is now the Czech Republic, Schindler began the war as an opportunist, exploiting Jewish labour to enrich himself under Nazi rule. However, as he witnessed the atrocities of the Holocaust, Schindler's conscience awakened, and he used his wealth and influence to shield his Jewish workers from certain death.

His journey from complicit profiteer, to moral hero, is a powerful testament to the capacity for change, even in the darkest circumstances. Schindler's story challenges us to examine our own choices, and to consider the moments when we are called to stand against injustice.

The Ground from Which It Grew: A World of Injustice and Opportunity

The early 1940s were a time of terror and brutality for Europe's Jewish population. In Nazi-occupied Poland, Jewish communities were torn apart, with millions sent to ghettos, forced labour camps, and extermination camps. Schindler, initially driven by personal gain, seized the opportunity to acquire a Jewish-owned enamelware factory in Kraków. He employed

Jewish workers, not out of compassion, but because their forced labour was cheaper and more accessible under Nazi policies.

At first, Schindler thrived in this system, enjoying wealth and status as a collaborator. But, as he witnessed the liquidation of the Kraków Ghetto and the inhumanity of the Nazi regime, Schindler's perspective shifted. The horror he saw forced him to confront his complicity, sparking a transformation that would define his legacy.

Are there situations in your life where you've Prioritised personal gain over doing what's right?

Sowing the Seeds of Mistake

Schindler's greatest mistake was his initial complicity in the Nazi system. By taking advantage of forced Jewish labour, he actively participated in a regime that dehumanised and destroyed lives. He saw his workers as tools for profit, not as individuals with inherent dignity. This moral blindness, while common in such an oppressive system, was a profound failure to recognise humanity in others.

However, Schindler's story is not one of unredeemed guilt. Once he saw the depth of the Nazi atrocities, he could no longer ignore his role. Instead, he took responsibility for the lives of his workers, using wealth, connections, and personal risk, to protect them from deportation and death.

Are there moments in your life where you've failed to recognise the humanity of others? How can you take steps to correct those mistakes?

Reaping What Was Sown

As the Holocaust intensified, Schindler's factory became a haven for Jews at risk of extermination. He bribed Nazi officials, falsified documents, and convinced authorities that his workers were essential to the war effort –

all to save lives. When the Nazis ordered the evacuation of Kraków's Jews to Auschwitz, Schindler took extraordinary risks to relocate his factory to Burnitz, creating the famous Schindler's List to protect over 1,200 people.

By the end of the war, Schindler had spent his fortune shielding his workers. He emerged penniless, but with a legacy of heroism. Despite his post-war struggles, the gratitude of those he saved ensured his place in history. In 1963, he was honoured as Righteous Among the Nations, and his story became immortalised in literature and film.

Are you willing to sacrifice personal comfort to stand up for what's right?

Harvesting the Lessons

Oskar Schindler began as a businessman who sought to profit from World War II, using forced Jewish labour to benefit his factories. However, as he witnessed the horrors of the Holocaust, he made a life-altering choice. Schindler risked his wealth, position, and safety to protect the lives of over 1,000 Jewish workers, ultimately saving them from certain death.

Schindler's story demonstrates the transformative power of conscience and moral courage. It reminds us that even those who have made questionable choices in the past can choose to act with integrity and compassion when faced with injustice.

The lessons of Schindler's life encourage us to recognise opportunities to make a difference, no matter our past. His actions challenge us to stand against wrongdoing and to use whatever influence we have to protect and uplift others in the face of adversity.

Here are three scenarios to reflect on, with reflections to help apply these lessons to your own life:

Scenario 1: Acknowledging Mistakes and Making Amends

You've recently been part of a disagreement or situation where, upon reflection, you realise you may have been in the wrong. While it feels uncomfortable, you sense that addressing the issue could improve the relationship or situation.

Reflection Questions:

- Are you open to acknowledging mistakes, even when it's difficult?

- How might avoiding accountability affect your relationships or personal growth?

- What steps could you take to make amends and move forward?

Scenario 2: Showing Empathy in Difficult Situations

You've encountered someone – perhaps a colleague, family member, or acquaintance – who has been difficult to deal with due to stress, differing opinions, or past conflicts. While it's tempting to dismiss their behaviour, you sense an opportunity to show empathy and connect on a deeper level.

Reflection Questions:

- How do you typically respond to people who challenge or frustrate you?

- What might change if you paused to recognise their humanity and understand their perspective?

- How can you demonstrate empathy in this situation, even if it feels inconvenient?

Scenario 3: Believing in Redemption and Taking a Stand

You've made a choice in the past that doesn't reflect who you want to be today. While you've grown since then, the mistake still weighs on you, and you wonder if it's too late to make amends or change the narrative.

Reflection Questions:

- Do you believe in the possibility of personal redemption, even after significant missteps?

- How could taking responsibility for your past choices help you grow and inspire others?

- What's one actionable step you can take today to move toward a sense of redemption – whether by forgiving yourself, apologizing, or making a positive change?

Final Reflection

Schindler's life shows that it's never too late to acknowledge mistakes, act with empathy, and strive for redemption. As you reflect, ask yourself:

- How might choosing empathy and accountability transform your relationships?
- What actions could you take today to move closer to the person you aspire to be?

Tilling the Soil of Reflection

Oskar Schindler's story reminds us that no matter how far we've strayed, redemption is always within reach. His journey compels us to examine our own actions and choices: Are we prioritising personal gain at the expense of others, or are we striving to use our influence to make a meaningful impact? Are we prepared to take bold, selfless risks to protect or uplift others, even when it challenges our comfort or security?

Breaking New Ground

Imagine a skilled artist, working tirelessly on a masterpiece. The artist carefully selects each colour, adjusts the brush strokes, and pours passion into every detail. But as time passes, the masterpiece begins to shift – the artist's vision changes, the world outside evolves, and the masterpiece no longer resonates in the same way.

Oskar Schindler's life mirrors this metaphor. His work, initially motivated by self-interest, gradually transformed into an act of profound moral courage, creating a legacy far beyond his original intentions.

Schindler, a businessman and war profiteer, used his position to save the lives of over 1,000 Jews during the Holocaust. Initially driven by profit, he later became a hero – his factory serving as a sanctuary for those in danger.

However, Schindler's journey wasn't without its own internal conflict. His shift from self-interest to altruism was not immediate, and he faced deep personal struggles in confronting the enormity of the atrocities around him. Like an artist refining their work, Schindler's transformation was shaped by his growing awareness of the human cost of his actions and the moral responsibility he held.

Have you ever experienced a shift in your values, realising that your actions were not aligned with your true purpose? Schindler's story asks us to reflect: Are we willing to confront our own mistakes and change the course of our lives to make a meaningful impact?

Cultivating Growth

Oskar Schindler's story is one of profound transformation – one man's journey from self-interest to selflessness. His actions reflect the power of Recognising the greater good, even in the face of overwhelming adversity.

Key Takeaways:

- **Redemption Through Action**: No matter the past, it's never too late to change and act in ways that reflect our values. Schindler's transformation shows us that redemption is possible through meaningful action.
- **Courage to Confront Reality**: Growth often requires us to face uncomfortable truths. Schindler's courage to act in the face of moral dilemmas challenges us to do the same in our lives.
- **The Power of Sacrifice**: Schindler's selflessness required personal sacrifice – financial, emotional, and physical. True growth sometimes means giving up something of ourselves for the benefit of others.

True growth is the willingness to confront our flaws, reassess our values, and change the course of our lives in pursuit of something greater than ourselves. Schindler's journey teaches us that transformation is possible, even for those who initially act from self-interest, as long as they choose to step into a larger moral responsibility.

MISTAKES ARE LIKE FERTILISER

So, here's your challenge: Are you ready to confront areas of your life where your actions don't align with your true values? How can you begin to make choices that reflect the impact you want to have on the world?

Growth isn't just about success – it's about evolving into the person you are meant to be and making choices that leave a lasting, positive legacy for others. Like Schindler, true growth is about Recognising the power of transformation and embracing the courage to act on it.

PLANTING STAGE 15

Alfred Nobel – The Legacy of Redemption

Quote: "I wish to leave behind me a world that is better than the one I found."
– Alfred Nobel

Image: Alfred Nobel (c. 1883). Public domain via Wikimedia Commons.

MISTAKES ARE LIKE FERTILISER

Before You Read:

What would you do if the world remembered you for the worst thing you created? Nobel's story shows what happens when someone rewrites their ending. His transformation has echoes in Jobs (Chapter 8) and Schindler (Chapter 14), but also stands in contrast to Ludwig II (Chapter 5), who never got that chance.

Breaking Ground: The Inventor of Dynamite

Alfred Nobel, born in 1833 in Stockholm, Sweden, was an inventor, chemist, and businessman whose most famous creation, dynamite, transformed industries like mining and construction – and sadly, warfare. Nobel's inventive mind led to over 350 patents, but none had the same global impact, or controversy, as dynamite.

In the 19th century, dynamite was a game changer. It made large construction projects, like railways and tunnels, possible. However, its use in warfare brought devastation, something Nobel never intended. Over time, instead of being known for progress, Nobel became linked with death and destruction.

The turning point in his life came when a French newspaper mistakenly published his obituary instead of his brother's. The obituary condemned him as a "merchant of death", stating that Nobel had made a fortune by inventing ways to kill people faster. This harsh judgment shook him deeply and made him re-evaluate how he wanted to be remembered.

The Ground from Which It Grew: The Industrial Age and Its Discontents

Nobel invented dynamite in 1867, during a time of rapid industrial growth. His creation was a key to unlocking the potential of large infrastructure projects, enabling faster, safer construction.

However, it was also adapted for military purposes, becoming a tool of war. What Nobel had envisioned as a force for good, was being used to destroy lives.

His family's involvement in the arms industry was well-established – Nobel's father had developed underwater mines, and Alfred himself had a number of explosive patents. Despite this, Nobel saw himself as a man of peace, and the realisation that his most famous invention was responsible for violence troubled him deeply.

The French newspaper's obituary forced Nobel to face a difficult truth: the world saw him as a man of destruction, not progress. This moment prompted him to take action and rewrite his legacy.

Are there actions or decisions in your life that could be interpreted differently than you intended? How might you proactively shape the way others perceive your contributions?

Sowing the Seeds of Mistake

Alfred Nobel's error wasn't the creation of dynamite itself, but underestimating how it would be misused. While he saw its potential for good, he overlooked how easily it could be turned into a weapon. Like many inventors, he was focused on the promise of progress, but didn't fully consider the darker side of human nature.

Dynamite, meant to build, was being used to destroy. Nobel was faced with the moral burden of his invention's impact. The newspaper obituary highlighted how the public perceived him – not as a brilliant scientist, but as a profiteer of death.

This realisation drove Nobel to think deeply about how he could change the narrative surrounding his life and work.

Are there unintended consequences of your actions or decisions that you need to address? What steps can you take to minimise harm or align your actions with your values?

Reaping What Was Sown

The obituary calling him the "merchant of death" was a wake-up call for Nobel. Realising his legacy could be defined by destruction, he decided to take action. In 1895, a year before his death, Nobel signed his final will, dedicating most of his fortune to establishing the Nobel Prizes. These prestigious awards would honour those who made exceptional contributions to physics, chemistry, medicine, literature, and peace.

The Nobel Peace Prize, in particular, was a direct response to his inner struggle over dynamite's deadly use. Nobel hoped to shift the world's view of his legacy from one of violence to one of progress, peace, and human advancement.

Nobel's decision paid off. Today, the Nobel Prizes are among the world's most respected awards, synonymous with excellence and positive contributions to humanity. The fact that Nobel's name is now associated with promoting peace and progress is a testament to his ability to reflect on his life, and change his legacy.

Are you actively working to leave behind a legacy that aligns with your values? What small adjustments could you make now to ensure your life's impact reflects your intentions?

Harvesting the Lessons

Alfred Nobel's life reveals the profound impact of reflection and the opportunity to reshape one's legacy. Known as the inventor of dynamite, Nobel was shocked to read his own premature obituary titled "The Merchant of Death", condemning him for profiting from explosives used in war. Determined to change how he would be remembered, Nobel created the Nobel Prizes, celebrating achievements in peace, science, and literature.

Nobel's story teaches us that it's never too late to redefine how the world sees us – or how we see ourselves. Mistakes and missteps do not have to define your legacy; instead, they can inspire growth and positive action.

These lessons resonate today, urging us to consider the long-term impact of our actions and how we can use our talents to contribute meaningfully to others. Nobel's journey reminds us that it's not about how you start, but how you choose to finish.

Here are three scenarios to reflect on, with reflections to help apply these lessons to your own life:

Scenario 1: Considering the Ripple Effects of Your Actions

You've made a decision or taken an action that seemed straightforward at the time, but you're beginning to notice how it's impacting others in ways you didn't anticipate.

Reflection Questions:

- How often do you pause to consider the unintended consequences of your actions?

- What steps can you take to align your decisions with your values and ensure they have a positive impact?

- How might reflecting on the ripple effects of your choices help you make better decisions in the future?

Scenario 2: Reflecting on Your Legacy

You've been thinking about the impact you're making in your personal or professional life. While you're proud of certain achievements, you wonder if there's more you can do to align your daily actions with the legacy you want to leave behind.

Reflection Questions:

- If someone described your life today, how closely would it align with how you want to be remembered?

- What values or aspirations do you want your legacy to reflect?

- What's one way you can start taking steps to ensure your actions contribute to the legacy you envision?

Scenario 3: Taking Responsibility and Making Amends

You've recently noticed a situation where your actions, intentionally or unintentionally, caused harm or misunderstanding. While addressing it feels uncomfortable, you realise that taking responsibility could repair relationships and foster trust.

Reflection Questions:

- How do you typically respond when faced with the unintended consequences of your actions?

- How might acknowledging responsibility strengthen your relationships or reputation?

- What's one step you can take today to address this situation, whether through an apology, making amends, or adjusting your approach?

Final Reflection

Nobel's story reminds us that it's never too late to change the course of our lives or to build a legacy aligned with our values. As you reflect, consider:

- How can taking responsibility for your actions lead to personal growth and stronger connections?
- What steps can you take today to create a lasting, positive impact on the people and world around you?

ALFRED NOBEL – THE LEGACY OF REDEMPTION

Tilling the Soil of Reflection

Alfred Nobel's story reminds us that it's never too late to take responsibility for our actions, and change the course of our lives. His creation of the Nobel Prizes transformed his legacy from one of destruction to one of peace and progress.

What do you want your legacy to be? Are you aware of how your actions may impact others, and are you ready to take responsibility for them?

Breaking New Ground

Imagine a rescue dog that was once abandoned and forgotten, wandering alone, unsure of where to go, or whom to trust. Over time, however, the dog is rescued, given care, and begins to trust again. It finds purpose, loyalty, and strength, becoming a companion who not only brings joy, but also courage and resilience to those around it. Alfred Nobel's life mirrors this transformation – a man who, like a rescue dog, was initially misunderstood and burdened by the weight of his own creations, only to eventually find redemption through self-awareness and purposeful action.

Nobel, the inventor of dynamite, initially created something that could be used for both construction and destruction. At first, he was known for his explosive inventions, which were seen as tools of violence.

However, when he read an obituary that referred to him as the "merchant of death" after his brother's passing, he was forced to confront the impact of his legacy. Like a rescue dog realising its worth after a painful past, Nobel redirected his wealth and influence, using it to establish the Nobel Prizes – awards that would celebrate peace, innovation, and humanitarian efforts.

Have you ever had a moment of reckoning where you realised the impact of your actions? Nobel's story asks us to consider: How can we use our past, even our mistakes, to create a future that is more meaningful and aligned with our values?

Cultivating Growth

Alfred Nobel's life illustrates that our past does not have to define our future. Like a rescue dog who learns to trust again and become a loyal companion, Nobel found redemption by aligning his resources with causes that could promote peace and benefit humanity.

Key Takeaways:

- **Embrace Redemption**: No matter the past, we have the power to redirect our efforts towards positive change. Like the rescue dog, we can rebuild trust and find a new purpose.
- **Use Past Mistakes for Growth**: Mistakes and missteps don't define us – they can guide us toward a more meaningful future. Nobel transformed his legacy by using his wealth for good.
- **Purpose Over Legacy**: True growth comes from aligning our actions with our values. Nobel's redirection of his focus from destruction to peace teaches us that we can always choose a path of greater purpose.

True growth isn't just about the choices we make in the moment – it's about learning from our past, finding redemption, and using our experiences to create something that serves a greater good. Nobel's shift from being seen as a creator of destruction, to a patron of peace, shows us that no matter where we start, we have the power to change the course of our lives and legacy.

So, here's your challenge: Are you willing to confront your past, learn from it, and use it to make a meaningful change in your life and in the world? How can you redirect your energy, like a rescue dog who finds new purpose, toward something that truly aligns with your values?

Growth is about more than just surviving – it's about finding a new direction, using our past to inform a better future, and helping others along the way.

CONCLUSION
Cultivating Your Own Growth

"Mistakes are like fertiliser – you can choose to let them grow you or kill you." – Tyson Roberts

Throughout this book, we've explored the lives of individuals who faced setbacks, failures, and moral dilemmas. Some were crushed by the weight of their choices, while others used their mistakes as stepping stones to growth and transformation. Whether it was a catastrophic error, a personal failing, or unchecked ambition, their stories offer invaluable lessons about reflection, resilience, and redemption.

So, what can we take away from these stories? The core message is simple yet profound: mistakes don't define us – our response to them does. Every error, failure, or wrong turn, holds the potential to fertilise our growth. It's up to us to decide how we'll use the experiences we've gained to shape the future we want to create.

Reflecting on Your Own Journey

As we've seen in these chapters, mistakes are inevitable. From Alfred Nobel's efforts to rewrite his legacy to Steve Jobs' ability to learn and return stronger, no one is immune to failure. The difference lies in how these individuals responded.

Are you taking time to reflect on your mistakes and learn from them? What steps can you take today to turn those lessons into growth opportunities?

Mistakes are not the end – they are part of your story. Use them to create a narrative of transformation and resilience.

Perspective Matters: One of the key takeaways from these stories is that growth begins with how we perceive failure. Instead of viewing mistakes as barriers, consider them stepping stones to greater understanding. Shifting your mindset is the first step in transforming setbacks into successes.

Ask yourself: How do you view your own failures? Are they obstacles, or do you see them as opportunities to grow?

Breaking the Cycle of Repeating Mistakes

The stories of individuals like Richard Nixon and Empress Dowager Cixi remind us that failure often becomes a cycle when we refuse to learn from it. Breaking this cycle requires humility – the courage to acknowledge where we've gone wrong and the determination to seek a better way forward.

Are there patterns in your life where mistakes keep repeating? What lessons are you resisting, and how can you begin to address them?

Recognising these patterns is the first step to breaking them. Be willing to look inward and use those lessons to shape a different future.

Planting the seed: While reflection is important, growth ultimately depends on action. Alfred Nobel could have stayed mired in guilt, but he took bold steps to shift his legacy. What action can you take to break free from repeated mistakes?

Ask yourself: What patterns in your life are holding you back? What small step could you take today to interrupt them?

The Courage to Forgive Yourself

One of the hardest lessons to embrace is the importance of self-forgiveness. Many of the figures in this book faced profound guilt over their actions, yet those who grew the most found ways to forgive themselves and move forward. Oskar Schindler turned his guilt into action; Alfred Nobel transformed his remorse into a legacy of peace.

Ask yourself: Are you holding onto guilt from past mistakes? How might forgiving yourself free you to grow and improve?

Self-forgiveness doesn't mean ignoring responsibility – it means acknowledging your mistakes, learning from them, and allowing yourself to move on. Growth cannot happen while you're still weighed down by the past.

Planting the seed: Identify one mistake or regret you're holding onto. Reflect on what you've learned from it and take one small step toward releasing it.

Building Strength Through Vulnerability

The stories in this book show that strength isn't about perfection – it's about the willingness to be vulnerable. Steve Jobs' ability to admit failure and return to Apple stronger than ever, or Alfred Nobel's courage to reshape his legacy, remind us that vulnerability is a key to growth.

Ask yourself: Are you open about your mistakes with others, or are you hiding behind an image of perfection? How might being vulnerable help, you connect more deeply with those around you?

Sharing your struggles not only helps you grow but also inspires others. Vulnerability is a bridge that connects us and reminds us that we're not alone in our failures.

Planting the seed: This week, share one lesson you've learned from a past mistake with someone you trust. Use it as an opportunity to deepen your connection and inspire them with your story of growth.

The Courage to Change

Oskar Schindler's decision to save lives, Alfred Nobel's transformation into a benefactor of peace, and Steve Jobs' evolution as a leader all demonstrate that change is possible, no matter how late or challenging.

Are you willing to make changes in your life, even if they're uncomfortable? What would it take to embrace a new path and redefine your story?

Change requires courage, honesty, and a willingness to act. But, as these stories have shown, it can lead to transformation – not just for you, but for the lives you impact.

Ask yourself: What is one area of your life where you need to embrace change? How can you take the first step toward a new path?

Your Own Fertiliser for Growth

Now, it's your turn. Think about the lessons in this book and how they apply to your life. Are you using your mistakes as opportunities for growth, or are you letting them hold you back?

Ask yourself: What lessons have my mistakes taught me? How can I use those lessons to build a future that aligns with my values and aspirations?

Keep these principles in mind as you move forward:

1. Reflect on your mistakes and understand them deeply.
2. Learn from those mistakes and extract their lessons.
3. Take action to make meaningful changes.
4. Forgive yourself and focus on progress, not perfection.

Mistakes, like fertiliser, can either nourish your growth or stifle it. It's your choice how to use them.

Planting the seed: Remember that your growth is not just for your benefit. The way you handle mistakes and challenges can inspire others, just as the stories in this book have inspired you.

Ask yourself: Who in your life might benefit from seeing your courage to grow and change?

A Call to Authenticity

One of the greatest challenges faced by the individuals in this book was remaining true to themselves amidst their failures. Authenticity – the courage to own your mistakes and use them as fuel for growth – is rare but essential.

Are you living authentically, or are you hiding behind success and perfection? How can you embrace your imperfections and inspire others through your growth?

In a world that glorifies success and hides failures, be the one who turns mistakes into opportunities for growth. True pioneers aren't those who avoid failure, but those who lead with honesty, resilience, and transformation.

Ask yourself: How can embracing authenticity and imperfection make you stronger? What might you inspire in others by leading with honesty and vulnerability?

Final Reflection: Redefining Failure

Failure isn't the end; it's part of the process. Whether it's learning forgiveness, like Mandela, bouncing back from disaster, like Churchill, or taking bold risks, like Musk, the stories in this book show that growth and redemption are always possible.

As you close this book, take a moment to reflect on your own journey. What mistakes have shaped you? What lessons have they taught you? And most importantly, how will you use those lessons to cultivate the best version of yourself?

Mistakes are like fertiliser – you can choose to let them grow you or kill you. Now, it's your turn. What will you choose?

REFERENCES

For those who wish to explore more about the people and events discussed in this book, below are key resources – books, articles, and documentaries – offering further information:

Chapter 1 — Ned Kelly

Biography

- Ian Jones, *Ned Kelly: A Short Life*
- Peter Carey, *True History of the Kelly Gang*
- Ian MacFarlane, *The Kelly Gang Unmasked*

Screen — Drama / Biopic

- *Ned Kelly* (2003)
- *The Last Outlaw* (TV Mini-Series)

Screen — Documentary

- *Outlaws of the Australian Bush*

Podcasts

- Forgotten Australia – "The Last Stand of Ned Kelly"

- Australian True Crime – "Bushrangers: Ned Kelly"
- History Lab – "Ned Kelly's Armour"

Digital Media & Online Exhibitions

- State Library of Victoria – Ned Kelly Collection
- National Museum of Australia – Kelly Gang Armour Display
- Public Record Office Victoria – Ned Kelly Trial Documents

Museums & Heritage Sites

- Ned Kelly Museum (Glenrowan, Victoria)
- Old Melbourne Gaol (Melbourne, Victoria)
- Beechworth Historic Courthouse (Beechworth, Victoria)

Chapter 2 — Napoleon Bonaparte

Biography

- Andrew Roberts, *Napoleon: A Life*
- Christopher Herold, *Napoleon and His Court*
- Philip Dwyer, *Napoleon: The Path to Power 1769–1799*

Historical & Cultural Analysis

- David G. Chandler, *The Campaigns of Napoleon*

Screen — Drama / Biopic

- *Napoleon* (2002, TV Mini-Series)

Screen — Documentary

- *Austerlitz: Napoleon's Greatest Victory*

REFERENCES

Podcasts

- The Age of Napoleon Podcast – "Napoleon's Rise"
- History Extra – "Napoleon: Man or Myth?"
- Revolutions Podcast – "The Napoleonic Wars"

Digital Media & Online Exhibitions

- Fondation Napoléon Digital Archives
- Musée de l'Armée (Paris) — Online Collection
- British Museum — Napoleonic Artefacts

Museums & Heritage Sites

- Les Invalides / Musée de l'Armée (Paris, France)
- Napoleon's Tomb (Paris, France)
- Château de Malmaison (Rueil-Malmaison, France)

Chapter 3 — Richard Nixon

Biography

- Rick Perlstein, *Nixonland*
- Carl Bernstein & Bob Woodward, *All the President's Men*
- Stanley I. Kutler, *The Wars of Watergate*
- Tim Weiner, *One Man Against the World*

Screen — Drama / Biopic

- *Frost/Nixon* (2008)

Screen — Documentary

- *Watergate: Blueprint for a Scandal*

Podcasts

- Slow Burn – "Watergate"
- American Scandal – "Watergate"
- History Extra – "Richard Nixon and Watergate"

Digital Media & Online Exhibitions

- Nixon Presidential Library Digital Archives
- Miller Center — Nixon Oral Histories
- C-SPAN — Nixon Speeches Archive

Museums & Heritage Sites

- Richard Nixon Presidential Library and Museum (Yorba Linda, USA)
- National Archives — Watergate Exhibit (Washington, D.C., USA)
- Gerald R. Ford Presidential Museum (Grand Rapids, USA)

Chapter 4 — Diego Maradona

Biography

- Jimmy Burns, *Maradona: The Hand of God*
- Diego Maradona, *Touched by God*
- Luca Caioli, *Once Upon a Time in Naples*

Screen — Documentary

- *Diego Maradona* (2019)
- *The Two Escobars*
- *The Last Interview: Diego Maradona*

REFERENCES

Podcasts

- The Athletic Football Podcast – "Maradona Remembered"
- Hand of Pod – "Diego Maradona Tribute"
- These Football Times – "Maradona at Napoli"

Digital Media & Online Exhibitions

- FIFA Digital Archive — Maradona Highlights
- Napoli Official Website — Maradona Legacy
- AFA Museum Online — Maradona Artefacts

Museums & Heritage Sites

- Museo del Calcio (Florence, Italy)
- Boca Juniors Museum (Buenos Aires, Argentina)
- Diego Maradona Stadium (Naples, Italy)

Chapter 5 — King Ludwig II of Bavaria

Biography

- Christopher McIntosh, *The Swan King*
- Julius Desing, *King Ludwig II: His Life and Art*
- Greg King, *Ludwig II of Bavaria: A Life Between Reality and Fantasy*

Screen — Documentary

- *Visions of Ludwig II*
- *Neuschwanstein: Germany's Fairy Tale Castle*

Podcasts

- History Extra – "Ludwig II: Mad King or Visionary?"

- The History of Germany Podcast – "Ludwig II"
- Footnoting History – "The Swan King"

Digital Media & Online Exhibitions

- Bavarian Palace Department — Virtual Castle Tours
- German National Museum — Ludwig II Collection
- UNESCO World Heritage — Bavarian Castles

Museums & Heritage Sites

- Neuschwanstein Castle (Bavaria, Germany)
- Linderhof Palace (Bavaria, Germany)
- Herrenchiemsee Palace (Bavaria, Germany)

Chapter 6 — Elon Musk

Biography

- Ashlee Vance, *Elon Musk: Tesla, SpaceX, and the Quest for a Fantastic Future*
- Tim Higgins, *Power Play: Tesla, Elon Musk, and the Bet of the Century*
- Eric Berger, *Liftoff*

Historical & Cultural Analysis

- Peter Diamandis, *The Future Is Faster Than You Think*

Screen — Documentary

- *Elon Musk: The Real-Life Iron Man*
- *Elon Musk: Risk Taker*

REFERENCES

Podcasts

- The Tim Ferriss Show – "Inside the Mind of Elon Musk"
- Third Row Tesla Podcast – "Interview with Elon Musk"
- Business Wars – "Tesla vs. Detroit"

Digital Media & Online Exhibitions

- SpaceX Official Website — Launch Archives
- Tesla Official Website — Investor and Product Resources
- Boring Company Project Updates

Museums & Heritage Sites

- Smithsonian National Air and Space Museum (Washington, D.C., USA)
- California Science Center (Los Angeles, USA)
- Johnson Space Center (Houston, USA)

Chapter 7 — Mark Zuckerberg

Biography

- David Kirkpatrick, *The Facebook Effect*
- Steven Levy, *Facebook: The Inside Story*
- Sheera Frenkel & Cecilia Kang, *An Ugly Truth*

Historical & Cultural Analysis

- Jaron Lanier, *Ten Arguments for Deleting Your Social Media Accounts Right Now*
- Roger McNamee, *Zucked*

Screen — Drama / Biopic

- *The Social Network* (2010)

Screen — Documentary

- *The Great Hack* (2019)
- *The Social Dilemma* (2020)
- *Inside Facebook: Secrets of the Social Network* (2018)

Podcasts

- The Daily – "The Facebook Whistleblower"
- Recode Decode – "Mark Zuckerberg on the Future of Facebook"
- Pivot – "Facebook's Big Problems"

Digital Media & Online Exhibitions

- Meta Newsroom
- Facebook Transparency Center
- Internet Archive – Facebook Interface Evolution

Museums & Heritage Sites

- Computer History Museum (Mountain View, USA)
- Smithsonian National Museum of American History (Washington, D.C., USA)

Chapter 8 — Steve Jobs

Biography

- Walter Isaacson, *Steve Jobs*
- Brent Schlender & Rick Tetzeli, *Becoming Steve Jobs*

REFERENCES

- Jay Elliot, *The Steve Jobs Way*

Historical & Cultural Analysis

- Ken Segall, *Insanely Simple*
- Adam Lashinsky, *Inside Apple*

Screen — Drama / Biopic

- *Steve Jobs* (2015)
- *Jobs* (2013)

Screen — Documentary

- *Steve Jobs: The Lost Interview* (2012)
- *Steve Jobs: Billion Dollar Hippy* (2011)
- *Steve Jobs: One Last Thing* (2011)

Podcasts

- How I Built This – "Apple: Steve Jobs"
- Business Wars – "Apple vs. Microsoft"
- The Tim Ferriss Show – "Lessons from Steve Jobs"

Digital Media & Online Exhibitions

- Apple Keynote Archives
- Smithsonian Oral History Interview (1995)
- Stanford Commencement Address (2005)

Museums & Heritage Sites

- Apple Park Visitor Center (Cupertino, USA)
- Computer History Museum (Mountain View, USA)
- Jobs' Childhood Home (Los Altos, USA)

Chapter 9 — Empress Dowager Cixi

Biography

- Jung Chang, *The Concubine Who Launched Modern China*
- Sterling Seagrave, *Empress Dowager Cixi*
- Laura Tyson Li, *Madame Chiang Kai-shek*

Historical & Cultural Analysis

- Sterling Seagrave, *Dragon Lady*
- Susan L. Shirk, *China: Fragile Superpower*
- Jonathan Spence, *The Search for Modern China*

Screen — Documentary

- *Cixi: The Iron Empress of China*
- *China: A Century of Revolution* (1989)
- *China's Last Empire: The Glory and Fall of the Qing*

Podcasts

- The China History Podcast – "Empress Dowager Cixi"
- Emperors of China Podcast – "Cixi and the End of the Qing"
- History Extra – "Reassessing the Empress Dowager Cixi"

Digital Media & Online Exhibitions

- The Palace Museum — Digital Collections
- British Museum — Qing Dynasty Collection
- Smithsonian Freer & Sackler Galleries Online

Museums & Heritage Sites

- The Summer Palace (Beijing, China)
- The Forbidden City / Palace Museum (Beijing, China)
- The Eastern Qing Tombs (Zunhua, China)

Chapter 10 — Marie Curie

Biography

- Susan Quinn, *Marie Curie: A Life*
- Eve Curie, *Madame Curie*
- Barbara Goldsmith, *Obsessive Genius*

Historical & Cultural Analysis

- Kate Moore, *Radium Girls*
- Naomi Pasachoff, *Marie Curie and the Science of Radioactivity*

Screen — Drama / Biopic

- *Radioactive* (2019)
- *Madame Curie* (1943)

Screen — Documentary

- *Marie Curie: The Courage of Knowledge* (2016)
- *Marie Curie: The Woman Who Changed the World*
- *PBS Nova — Einstein's Big Idea*

Podcasts

- The History Chicks – "Marie Curie"
- Stuff You Missed in History Class – "Marie Curie"

- The Science History Podcast – "Marie Curie's Legacy"

Digital Media & Online Exhibitions

- Pierre and Marie Curie Museum — Virtual Tour
- Nobel Prize Official Site — Marie Curie Profile
- Smithsonian Libraries — Marie Curie Archive

Museums & Heritage Sites

- Musée Curie (Paris, France)
- Curie Institute (Paris, France)
- Curie's Childhood Home (Warsaw, Poland)

Chapter 11 — Akio Morita

Biography

- Akio Morita, *Made in Japan*
- Akio Morita & Edwin M. Reingold, *The Sony Vision*
- Robert Sobel, *Sony: The Company and Its Founders*

Historical & Cultural Analysis

- Kaori Shoji, *Innovation Nation*
- John Nathan, *Sony: The Private Life*

Screen — Documentary

- *Akio Morita: Global Visionary*
- *The Walkman Revolution*
- *NHK World — Japanology Plus: Sony*

Podcasts

- Business Wars – "Sony vs. Nintendo"
- The Asian Review of Books Podcast – "The Legacy of Sony"
- Cold Call – "Sony's Bet on Innovation"

Digital Media & Online Exhibitions

- Sony Global Archives
- NHK Digital Archives — Sony Features
- IEEE Global History Network — Sony Entry

Museums & Heritage Sites

- Sony Archives (Tokyo, Japan)
- Miraikan (Tokyo, Japan)
- Akio Morita Library (Sony HQ)

Chapter 12 — Nelson Mandela

Biography

- Nelson Mandela, *Long Walk to Freedom*
- Anthony Sampson, *Mandela: The Authorised Biography*
- Nelson Mandela, *Conversations with Myself*

Historical & Cultural Analysis

- Njabulo Ndebele, *The Cry of Winnie Mandela*

Screen — Drama / Biopic

- *Invictus* (2009)

Screen — Documentary

- *Mandela: Long Walk to Freedom*

Podcasts

- History Extra – "Nelson Mandela's Legacy"
- BBC Witness History – "Nelson Mandela"
- The Documentary Podcast (BBC) – "Mandela: The Making of a Leader"

Digital Media & Online Exhibitions

- Nelson Mandela Foundation Digital Archive
- South African History Online — Mandela Collection
- Robben Island Museum Virtual Tour

Museums & Heritage Sites

- Apartheid Museum (Johannesburg, South Africa)
- Robben Island Museum (Cape Town, South Africa)
- Nelson Mandela Museum (Mthatha, South Africa)

Chapter 13 — Winston Churchill

Biography

- Andrew Roberts, *Churchill: Walking with Destiny*
- Boris Johnson, *The Churchill Factor*
- Erik Larson, *The Splendid and the Vile*

Historical & Cultural Analysis

- Winston S. Churchill, *Never Give In!*

REFERENCES

Screen — Drama / Biopic

- *Darkest Hour* (2017)
- *The Crown* (Season 1, Ep. 9)

Screen — Documentary

- *Churchill's Secret Agents: The New Recruits*
- *Winston Churchill: Walking with Destiny*

Podcasts

- The Rest is History – "Winston Churchill"
- BBC History Extra – "Churchill in War and Peace"
- We Have Ways of Making You Talk – "Churchill's WWII Leadership"

Digital Media & Online Exhibitions

- Churchill Archives Centre (Cambridge University)
- UK National Archives — Churchill Collection
- Imperial War Museums Digital Archive

Museums & Heritage Sites

- Churchill War Rooms (London, UK)
- Blenheim Palace (Woodstock, UK)
- Chartwell (Kent, UK)

Chapter 14 — Oskar Schindler

Biography

- Thomas Keneally, *Schindler's Ark*

- David M. Crowe, *Schindler and His List*

Historical & Cultural Analysis

- Gay Block, *Rescuers: Portraits of Moral Courage in the Holocaust*

Screen — Drama / Biopic

- *Schindler's List* (1993)

Screen — Documentary

- *Righteous Among the Nations – Oskar Schindler*
- *Voices from the List*

Podcasts

- Holocaust Encyclopedia – "Oskar Schindler"
- History Extra – "The True Story of Oskar Schindler"
- The Documentary (BBC) – "Schindler's Jews"

Digital Media & Online Exhibitions

- Yad Vashem — Oskar Schindler Archive
- US Holocaust Memorial Museum — Schindler Collection
- Spielberg Jewish Film Archive — Schindler's List Materials

Museums & Heritage Sites

- Oskar Schindler's Enamel Factory Museum (Kraków, Poland)
- Yad Vashem (Jerusalem, Israel)
- Holocaust Memorial Museum (Washington, D.C., USA)

REFERENCES

Chapter 15 — Alfred Nobel

Biography

- Kenne Fant, *Alfred Nobel: A Biography*
- Ragnar Sohlman, *Nobel: The Man and His Prizes*
- Tore Frängsmyr, *Alfred Nobel: His World and Legacy*

Historical & Cultural Analysis

- Burton Feldman, *The Nobel Prize: A History of Genius, Controversy, and Prestige*

Screen — Documentary

- *The Man Behind the Peace Prize*
- *The Merchant of Death is Dead*

Podcasts

- BBC World Service – "Alfred Nobel and the Peace Prize"
- Nobel Prize Conversations – "The Story of Alfred Nobel"
- History Extra – "The History of the Nobel Prize"

Digital Media & Online Exhibitions

- Nobel Prize Official Website — Alfred Nobel Archives
- Swedish Academy Digital Archives — Nobel Prize History
- Swedish National Museum of Science and Technology — Nobel Exhibits

Museums & Heritage Sites

- Nobel Prize Museum (Stockholm, Sweden)

MISTAKES ARE LIKE FERTILISER

- Alfred Nobel House (Karlskoga, Sweden)
- Alfred Nobel House (Björkborn, Sweden)

EXTRA RESOURCES

Why These Resources Matter

As you've journeyed through this book, you've seen how mistakes, setbacks, and personal struggles are an inevitable part of life. The individuals whose stories we've explored faced immense challenges, often requiring courage, reflection, and resilience to navigate their paths. But while their experiences can inspire and guide us, it's important to remember that personal growth is not a journey we must take alone.

The mental health support services included in this section are here to remind you that help is always available. Sometimes, facing mistakes and breaking patterns of failure requires more than self-reflection—it requires professional guidance, community support, and compassionate care. These resources are a bridge between the lessons of this book and the actionable steps you can take to cultivate growth in your own life.

Whether you're dealing with stress, anxiety, trauma, or the lingering weight of a past mistake, reaching out for support is a sign of strength, not weakness. Just as the figures in this book had mentors, allies, or turning points that shaped their journeys, these services are here to serve as your allies in times of need.

Growth, healing, and transformation often require more than insight; they demand practical tools and strategies tailored to your unique situation. These services can help you navigate your challenges with professional care and empower you to rewrite your story with resilience and purpose.

Let this final section serve as an invitation—to seek help when needed, to connect with others who can guide you, and to embrace the support systems that can foster your growth. You are not alone in your journey, and with the right resources, your mistakes truly can become the fertiliser for a life of authenticity, strength, and impact.

Below Are a Few Services, But Not Limited to These

The following list represents just a starting point—key services available in Australia designed to support your mental health and well-being. These organisations offer resources for a variety of needs, including stress management, trauma recovery, and professional counselling. While these services provide a strong foundation, they are by no means exhaustive.

Everyone's journey is unique, and you may find that additional local or specialised resources better suit your personal circumstances. I encourage you to explore what is available in your area and reach out to the service that feels right for you.

Remember, seeking help is a courageous and transformative step toward growth. These services are here to guide and support you as you navigate life's challenges and create a healthier, more fulfilling future.

CRISIS & RESILIENCE SUPPORT SERVICES

(All are free, confidential, and 24/7 unless otherwise noted)

Australia

- Beyond Blue – Mental health and resilience support. **www.beyondblue.org.au**
- Lifeline Australia – Crisis phone/text support. **www.lifeline.org.au**
- Head to Health – Government portal for trusted mental health resources. **www.headtohealth.gov.au**
- 13YARN – Crisis line for Aboriginal and Torres Strait Islander peoples. **www.13yarn.org.au**
- The Resilience Centre – Programs for bouncing back from adversity. **www.theresiliencecentre.com.au**

United States

- NAMI – Support groups, education, advocacy. **www.nami.org**
- 988 Suicide & Crisis Lifeline – Call or text 988. **www.988lifeline.org**

- Crisis Text Line – Text "HELLO" to 741741. www.crisistextline.org
- SAMHSA / FindTreatment.gov – Locate confidential mental health/substance use help. www.findtreatment.gov
- BetterHelp – Affordable online therapy. www.betterhelp.com

United Kingdom

- Mind (UK) – Helpline, local support, mental health resources. www.mind.org.uk
- Samaritans – Call 116 123 or email jo@samaritans.org. www.samaritans.org
- Hub of Hope – UK-wide support directory. www.hubofhope.co.uk
- CALM – Suicide prevention campaigns and helplines. www.thecalmzone.net
- The School of Life – Workshops on relationships and resilience. www.theschooloflife.com

International & Specialist Support

- IFRC Psychosocial Centre – Global crisis recovery resources. www.pscentre.org
- WHO Mental Health & Substance Use – Global health and coping tools. www.who.int/teams/mental-health-and-substance-use
- Disaster Distress Helpline (USA) – Call or text 1-800-985-5990
- Eating Disorders Victoria & Ngamai Wilam (Australia) – Multidisciplinary recovery programs
- Peer Support Apps (e.g. Fello) – Connect with trained peers for listening and guidance

MENTAL HEALTH SUPPORT SERVICES

Australia

1. **Beyond Blue**
   - **Focus:** Mental health support and resilience.
   - **Services:** 24/7 mental health support hotline, online forums, resources for anxiety and depression.
   - **Why it benefits:** Provides tools for dealing with failure, building resilience, and managing mental health.
   - **Website:** www.beyondblue.org.au

2. **Lifeline Australia**
   - **Focus:** Crisis support and suicide prevention.
   - **Services:** 24/7 crisis support, free and confidential phone and text services.
   - **Why it benefits:** Helps readers navigate emotional crises and overcome life's setbacks.
   - **Website:** www.lifeline.org.au

3. **The Resilience Centre**
   - **Focus:** Building personal resilience and emotional well-being.
   - **Services:** Counselling, workshops, and programs focused on bouncing back from adversity.
   - **Why it benefits:** Provides actionable strategies to turn setbacks into growth opportunities.
   - **Website:** www.theresiliencecentre.com.au

4. **Relationships Australia**
   - **Focus:** Relationships and personal development.
   - **Services:** Counselling, mediation, and relationship skills workshops.
   - **Why it benefits:** Supports readers looking to mend relationships affected by mistakes or failures.
   - **Website:** www.relationships.org.au

5. **Smiling Mind**
   - **Focus:** Mindfulness and emotional regulation.
   - **Services:** Free mindfulness meditation app and resources for individuals, schools, and workplaces.
   - **Why it benefits:** Helps readers cultivate a calm mindset to reflect and grow.
   - **Website:** www.smilingmind.com.au

United States

1. **National Alliance on Mental Illness (NAMI)**
   - **Focus:** Mental health advocacy and support.
   - **Services:** Free support groups, educational programs, and resources for individuals and families.

- **Why it benefits:** Helps readers address mental health struggles tied to failure or setbacks.
- **Website:** www.nami.org

2. **BetterHelp**
   - **Focus:** Accessible online counselling.
   - **Services:** Online therapy sessions with licensed professionals.
   - **Why it benefits:** Offers readers affordable and flexible mental health support.
   - **Website:** www.betterhelp.com

3. **Mindful.org**
   - **Focus:** Mindfulness and meditation for personal growth.
   - **Services:** Articles, courses, and guided meditations.
   - **Why it benefits:** Teaches techniques to manage stress and reflect on mistakes constructively.
   - **Website:** www.mindful.org

4. **Headspace**
   - **Focus:** Meditation and mental wellness.
   - **Services:** Guided meditations, sleep aids, and mindfulness practices.
   - **Why it benefits:** Supports readers in developing a growth-oriented mindset.
   - **Website:** www.headspace.com

5. **Crisis Text Line**
   - **Focus:** Immediate crisis support.
   - **Services:** 24/7 text-based support from trained crisis counsellors.

- **Why it benefits:** Provides a discreet, accessible option for readers in moments of emotional distress.
- **Website:** www.crisistextline.org
- **Text Line:** Text "HELLO" to 741741

United Kingdom

1. **Mind (UK)**
   - **Focus:** Mental health support and advocacy.
   - **Services:** Helplines, counselling resources, and local support groups.
   - **Why it benefits:** Helps readers manage the emotional toll of mistakes and setbacks.
   - **Website:** www.mind.org.uk

2. **Samaritans**
   - **Focus:** Crisis support and suicide prevention.
   - **Services:** 24/7 helpline, text support, and online chat.
   - **Why it benefits:** Offers a lifeline to readers navigating personal crises.
   - **Website:** www.samaritans.org

3. **The School of Life**
   - **Focus:** Emotional education and self-improvement.
   - **Services:** Workshops, books, and resources on relationships, careers, and resilience.
   - **Why it benefits:** Provides readers with tools to navigate emotional growth and relationships.
   - **Website:** www.theschooloflife.com

4. **CALM (Campaign Against Living Miserably)**
   - **Focus:** Mental health and suicide prevention for men and women.
   - **Services:** Helplines, campaigns, and community resources.
   - **Why it benefits:** Supports readers in addressing stigma and fostering mental well-being.
   - **Website:** www.thecalmzone.net

5. **Action for Happiness**
   - **Focus:** Promoting happiness and mental well-being.
   - **Services:** Local groups, courses, and practical guides for living a meaningful life.
   - **Why it benefits:** Encourages a positive approach to mistakes and personal growth.
   - **Website:** www.actionforhappiness.org

ABOUT THE AUTHOR

Tyson Roberts is a debut author, storyteller, and full-time truck driver with a passion for helping others embrace life's imperfections. With a deep belief that mistakes hold the seeds of transformation, Tyson has dedicated his writing to uncovering the lessons hidden in failure. Through relatable stories and reflective prompts, Tyson encourages readers to see mistakes not as failures but as opportunities for growth and reinvention.

The idea for *Mistakes Are Like Fertiliser* was born in July 2016 when Tyson created the quote: *"Mistakes are like fertiliser - you can choose to let them grow you or kill you."* This realisation wasn't born in a moment of triumph but from the aftermath of life-altering mistakes that forced him to pause, reflect, and rebuild. The concept grew out of raw honesty and hard-earned wisdom, becoming the foundation for a book that shows how mistakes - whether our own or those of others - can serve as powerful tools for transformation.

While Tyson's personal journey isn't the focus of *Mistakes Are Like Fertiliser*, his experiences have shaped his unique perspective. From childhood abuse to surviving near-death accidents, dying and coming back to life, to overcoming addiction, navigating financial struggles, and learning to rebuild after life's toughest moments, Tyson understands what it means to face failure head-on. These experiences have taught him that mistakes are universal, but how we respond to them determines whether they define us - or refine us.

In *Mistakes Are Like Fertiliser,* Tyson dives into the lives of historical and contemporary figures who made mistakes with far-reaching consequences. Some rose above their failures to achieve greatness, while others allowed their mistakes to lead to ruin. By examining their stories, Tyson offers readers practical lessons on accountability, resilience, and self-discovery. His conversational tone and down-to-earth approach make these lessons accessible and relatable, no matter where readers are on their own journeys.

Beyond the book, Tyson draws inspiration from his day-to-day life. Whether driving trucks, raising his children, or sharing laughs with his wife, he's committed to living authentically and fostering connection in his community. Tyson believes the power to change comes from listening to and learning from others with humility and an open heart. Through this lens, he uses his writing to encourage meaningful conversations and inspire readers to approach their own challenges with resilience and grace.

Tyson isn't a polished, untouchable figure - he's a fellow traveller on the road of life, navigating its twists and turns just like everyone else. His writing is a reflection of that journey, offering readers a chance to learn from the past and grow into the future.

Join the Journey: Email Tyson at mistakesarelike@gmail.com or follow Tyson on social media @mistakesarelike. Come connect with the community on Facebook for more stories, lessons, and reflections about resilience, growth, and the power of embracing life's imperfections.

Tyson Roberts passionately believes that every story of growth begins with a mistake—and every mistake holds the potential to inspire transformation in ourselves and those around us.

www.ingramcontent.com/pod-product-compliance
Lightning Source LLC
Chambersburg PA
CBHW032110090426
42743CB00007B/303